KU-646-887

# Contents

*(Page numbers refer to Teacher's Notes. Worksheet references are given under 'Materials'.)*

# THE *ANTI-GRAMMAR* GRAMMAR BOOK

## A Teacher's Resource Book
## of discovery activities for grammar teaching

Nick Hall and
John Shepheard

**Addison Wesley Longman Limited,**
Edinburgh Gate
Harlow
Essex
CM20 2JE, England
*and Associated Companies throughout the world.*

© Longman Group UK Limited 1991
*All rights reserved; no part of this publication*
*may be reproduced, stored in a retrieval system,*
*or transmitted in any form or by any means, electronic,*
*mechanical, photocopying, recording, or otherwise,*
*without the prior written permission of the Publishers.*

First published 1991
Eighth impression 1997

Set in 10/11 Century Light
Produced through Longman Malaysia, GPS

ISBN 0 582 03390 X

## Copyright

### Acknowledgements

We would like to thank the Principal, staff and students of
Angloschool, London, without whose help this book would
be the poorer.

We are grateful to the following for permission to reproduce
copyright material;

BBC Enterprises Ltd for the article 'My Kind of Day' by
William Greaves from *Radio Times* 13–19 January 1990 (pub
BBC Magazines); The Guardian for an extract from the article
'Australia Mourns' from *The Guardian* 19.2.83; Penguin
Books Ltd for the adapted extracts 'The World Divorce
Record Holder', 'The Least Successful Target Practice', 'The
Least Alert Burglar', 'The Most Unsuccessful Prison Escape' &
'The Worst Bank Robbers' from *The Book of Heroic Failures*
by Stephen Pile (pub Viking, 1989), copyright © Stephen Pile,
1979, 1989; the author, Tim Radford for his adapted article
'Africa braces itself for new plague' from *The Guardian*
19.5.88; Robson Books Ltd for extracts from *Help! I'm a
Prisoner in a Toothpaste Factory* by John Antrobus; Scope
Features (Photographers Agents) Ltd for the extracts 'All Our
Yesterdays' & 'Legwork' from *TV Times* 9–15 April 1988; Solo
Syndication & Literary Agency Ltd for an extract from the
article 'Should we be proud of our British cool?' from
*Woman's Own* 9.4.88; Times Newspapers Ltd, London, for an
extract from the article 'Girl Had Bullet In Her Scalp' by Craig
Seeton from *The Times* 10.10.86; Transworld Publishers Ltd
& the author's agent for extracts & adapted extracts from *The
Book of Narrow Escapes* by Peter Mason (pub Corgi Books),
© Peter Mason 1984; the author, Michael White for his article
'US Telephone Thief Makes His Last Call' from *The Guardian*
31.8.88.

We are grateful to the following for permission to reproduce
cartoons and other copyright material;

Camera Press, page 141; Commercial Union Assurance, page
133; cartoon by Boris Drucker, © 1984, from *The New Yorker
Magazine*, Inc; Patrick Eagar Photography, page 146; Express
Newspapers/*Daily Star*, page 138; Friends of the Earth, page
153; *The Guardian*, page 148; London Theatre Guide, page
141; cartoons by Edward McLachlan from *The Book of
Narrow Escapes*, Peter Mason, Corgi Books, pages 127 and
135; Mirror Group Newspapers, cartoons from *Daily Mirror
Laughter Cartoons 4*, 1982, pages 91, 117, 118 and 121; News
International Newspapers/The Sun, page 138; Otto
Reisinger/Eurocartoon, page 83.

Designed by Ann Samuel
Illustrated by B.L. Kearley Ltd

## Section 3: Futures

| | | | | |
|---|---|---|---|---|
| 3.1 | How simple is the future simple? | Future simple | Highlighting the will/shall distinction | Upp.-int. – adv. 20 mins | **64** |
| 3.2 | Funny future | Future simple, *going to* future, present simple, present continuous | Presentation and summary of uses | Mid.-int. – adv. 50 mins | **64** |
| 3.3 | Journalist of the future | Future simple, *going to* future, present simple, present continuous | Controlled practice | Mid.-int. – adv. 40–50 mins | **66** |
| 3.4 | Double date | Future simple, *going to* future, present simple, present continuous | Information exchange | Int. – upp.-int. 40 mins | **67** |
| 3.5 | Anyone for cricket? | Future simple, *going to* future, present simple, present continuous | Correction of errors of use | Mid. int. – adv. 50 mins | **68** |
| 3.6 | Who will be dancing in the streets? | Future continuous | Correction of errors of form | Mid.-int. – upp.-int. 20–30 mins | **69** |
| 3.7 | Gilbert | Future continuous | Presentation | Upp.-int. – adv. 25 mins | **70** |
| 3.8 | Caribbean future | Future simple, future continuous | Summary of time reference/ use, contrast of verb forms | Upp.-int. – adv. 30 mins | **71** |
| 3.9 | Siesta | Future continuous | Controlled practice | Mid.-int. – upp.-int. 30 mins | **72** |
| 3.10 | The perfect future for the kangaroo? | Future perfect simple and continuous | Correction of errors of form | Upp.-int. – adv. 30 mins | **74** |
| 3.11 | 2001 and the ozone story | Future perfect simple | Presentation | Upp.-int. – adv. 30 mins | **75** |
| 3.12 | Ozone – a thing of the past or the future? | Future perfect simple, future simple | Summary of time reference/use, contrast of verb forms | Upp.-int. – adv. 25 mins | **76** |
| 3.13 | By the time you're 100… | Future perfect simple | Controlled practice | Int. – upp.-int. 20–30 mins | **78** |
| 3.14 | Problems, problems, problems! | Future perfect continuous | Presentation | Upp.-int. – adv. 30 mins | **79** |

# Introduction

## Anti-grammar grammar?

*The Anti-Grammar Grammar Book* certainly promotes grammar – the
investigation of rules of form and corresponding meanings in the language system.
It is *anti*-grammar in that it sets out to avoid *giving* students rules. Instead it
casts the students in the role of 'thinker', providing them with cognitive,
problem-solving tasks to discover grammatical rules and meanings for themselves.
The material does not say, 'Here is a rule and a meaning, learn them!' but rather,
'Here is a sample of English – discover the rules and meanings for yourself!'

   *The Anti-Grammar Grammar Book* also sets out to avoid the conventional
gap-fill and transformation exercises which proliferate in existing materials. Instead
it provides a variety of cognitive, involving, and creative activities to practise
language both in controlled and freer frameworks. The content of the exercises is
intended not just to present and practise language areas but to be of interest to the
student in its own right. All of the activities have been fully tried and tested in
classrooms.

## Content and organisation

*The Anti-Grammar Grammar Book* is a grammar resource book providing
alternative and supplementary material to present and practise verb forms in the
present, past, and future. Each resource activity consists of photocopiable student
material introduced by detailed teachers' notes in the first half of the book. The
teachers' notes contain aims, suggested levels and time frames, materials required,
step by step classroom procedure, and keys to the exercises.

   There are three sections:

1 **Presents**: Present simple, present continuous, present perfect simple, present
   perfect continuous

2 **Pasts**: Past simple, past continuous, past perfect simple, past perfect continuous

3 **Futures**: Future simple, future continuous, future perfect simple, future perfect
   continuous, present simple, present continuous, *going to*

The materials focus solely on these three areas for the sake of completeness and to
avoid providing a mere scrapbook of bits and pieces.

## Target students

The material is mainly intended for upper-intermediate and advanced students who
have met most of the tenses and verb forms of the language. The material acts as a
re-presentation in one block of the forms and meanings of each tense or verb form.
In this way the tenses or verb forms are reviewed for remedial purposes and to
give students an overall picture of the tense and verb form system. The material
would be suitable for students preparing for Cambridge First Certificate and for
those at a pre-Cambridge Proficiency stage. The exercises have also been used with
EFL teachers at trainee and post-experience levels.

## Role of the material in the course

*The Anti-Grammar Grammar Book* can be used on its own as a grammar course.
To this end, the activities and exercises are arranged in sequences moving from
presentation to production. A number of the exercises have been planned to be

worked through in tandem. This is normally the case when a particular tense/verb form has been initially presented and is then contrasted with another form. When this applies, mention is made in the teachers' notes – for example, uses of the present continuous are presented in contexts in 1.6 'We are continuing presently' (A), and then the uses are summarised and the present continuous contrasted with the present simple in 1.7 'We are continuing presently' (B). In this case it would, therefore, be difficult to do the second set of activities without completing the first.

Alternatively, *The Anti-Grammar Grammar Book* can be used selectively to supplement other course books which at the upper-intermediate to advanced level often lack the space necessary to provide sufficient material in grammatical areas, especially when remedial work becomes necessary.

## Form

The approach to form is through error correction. Common errors of form gathered from student classroom production are presented for examination and correction. Finally, meaningful summary tables are completed by the students. In this way the students collaborate in compiling their own reference tables.

## Meaning

The verb forms are presented in written contexts and students guided towards an understanding of concepts and use. The texts aim not simply to contextualise the verb forms but also to engage the students' interest. To this end the book includes articles about environmental issues, cartoons and humorous material, true stories of an unusual and intriguing nature, and items of cultural interest. As with the approach to form, students complete summary tables for their own future reference.

## Timelines

Classroom experience shows that diagrams and timelines can be a useful way of provoking discussion and exploring time reference. Interesting discussion areas come up. For example, is *She works in a bank* to be represented as a series of repeated actions or as a permanent state?

Timelines are included in the teachers' notes as part of an optional exercise. Two strategies are possible – either students can devise their own timelines and discuss them, or the teacher can put the suggested timelines on the board for students to match with the example sentences in the summary tables.

There are several different ways of representing verb forms – for an excellent discussion of the topic, see the section on Diagrams in Chapter 21 of *The English Verb* by Michael Lewis (LTP). We have adopted the following system:

| | | | |
|---|---|---|---|
| × | single event/action | He flew to Russia.<br><br>PAST　　　NOW　　FUTURE<br><br>　×　　　　⊢———— | (past simple) |
| × (×)(×) | event/action possibly repeated one or more times | He's been to Russia.<br><br>PAST　　　NOW　　FUTURE<br>?<br>× (×)(×)　　⊢———— | (present perfect) |

| | | | |
|---|---|---|---|
| × × × × × × | repeated action/permanent habit | He goes to Russia every month.<br><br>PAST　　NOW　　FUTURE<br>× × × \| × × × | (present simple) |
| ∿∿ | temporary state/event | He's flying to Russia at the moment.<br><br>PAST　　NOW　　FUTURE<br>∿∿∿∿\|∿∿∿∿ | (present continuous) |
| (x⌢x⌢x⌢x) | temporary repeated action/habit | He's flying to Russia a lot these days.<br><br>PAST　　NOW　　FUTURE<br>(x⌢x⌢x\|x⌢x⌢x) | (present continuous) |
| ————— | permanent state | He lives in Moscow.<br><br>PAST　　NOW　　FUTURE<br>———\|——— | (present simple) |
| ↓ | point of time | He landed in Moscow at four.<br><br>PAST　　NOW　　FUTURE<br>4<br>x　　　　\| | (past simple) |
| ∿∿∿↓ | period of time | He was flying for two hours.<br><br>PAST　　NOW　　FUTURE<br>2 HOURS<br>∿∿∿↓　　\| | (past continuous) |

When students are unfamiliar with timelines, examples could be given from the above list and then students could try drawing timelines for some of the other sentences. Alternatively, students can match the timelines to the sentences.

### Group discussion

There is a good deal of emphasis on pair and group discussion in the suggested procedures in the teachers' notes. We recommend that the teacher refrains from providing answers and solutions until the class has reached its own conclusions. In this way students have more involvement and responsibility for the learning process. We strongly advise that students complete the worksheets initially in *pencil* so that adjustments can be made later to provide a final record and summary of forms and meanings.

### Team games

We have included a number of game frameworks with points systems for some of the activities. This has been found to be very motivating with a lot of classes of all ages. However, where this approach does not suit particular groups, the activities can still be carried out by simply removing the competitive element.

## Error correction

We have recommended in the teachers' notes to productive and communicative exercises that errors made by students are noted down by the teacher and corrected with the students after the productive tasks have been completed. This is because we feel that it is probably not a good idea to interrupt an activity as long as communication is taking place. We suggest that one of the following procedures is adopted. During an activity the teacher can make a list of significant errors and especially those which concern the target language to be practised. This can be done down one side of a sheet of paper and then photocopied for distribution to the class who then try to correct the errors for homework or in class, writing the correction down the other side of the page. Alternatively, the errors can be written directly onto an OHP transparency and then displayed for the class to correct in pairs or groups. If an OHP is not available then the errors can be transcribed onto the board or written directly onto a large covered sheet of card. Another possibility is to note errors on slips of paper with the student's name and to give these to the relevant students at the end of the activity for self-correction.

## Time frames

Clearly, the suggested times for the exercises can only be approximate and the actual time taken will depend on the students, the size of class, time of the working day, and so on. Where class time is short, some of the exercises can be carried out for homework and then followed up and discussed later in class.

## Teacher training

The presentation and contrastive material has been found to be very effective for developing the language awareness of teacher trainees. It has been used with non-native speaker teachers, with native speaker trainees on initial training courses like RSA Cambridge Certificate in TEFLA courses, and on in-service training and post-experience courses like those leading to the RSA Cambridge Diploma in TEFLA. The exercises have a dual value in both extending language awareness and showing how such language areas can be presented at upper-intermediate and advanced levels.

In practice we have adopted two approaches. In the first case trainees were asked to work through the material as it stands. Alternatively, we have deleted the questions from the contexts or the contrastive sets of sentences and asked trainees to work out the basic uses of the verb forms unguided.

# Presents

## 1.1 Im Zoo

| | |
|---|---|
| VERB FORM | Present simple, present continuous |
| AIM | Correcting errors of form and use in the present simple and present continuous |
| LEVEL | Mid-intermediate to advanced |
| TIME | 30 minutes |
| MATERIALS | One copy of 'Im Zoo' for each student (page 83) |

IN CLASS

### A Previewing the cartoon

Ask students to imagine what the animals in a zoo would say about the visitors if they could speak. Elicit ideas from the class.

### B Correcting errors

1 Give each student a copy of 'Im Zoo' and ask them what is unusual about the situation in the zoo (i.e. the people and animals have swapped roles).

2 Ask them to read the speech bubbles to find mistakes in grammatical form, or use of the present simple and present continuous. Tell the class that some of the sentences are correct.

3 Students work individually and then compare answers in pairs or small groups.

4 As the students finish, and depending on class size, give individual students one or more of the fourteen answers. Students then mingle to check their answers.

VARIATION

Organise the class into teams of two to four students. Give them about ten minutes to work on the sentences. Teams take turns to select any of the sentences and win a point for identifying whether it is correct or incorrect, and a second point for correcting an error.

KEY

### B Correcting errors

1 Correct
2 Incorrect: *Do* you understand this? (However, this is acceptable as an expression of surprise.)
3 Correct
4 Incorrect: Look! There's the one who always *gives* us food.
5 Incorrect: The ones with cameras always *find* us so interesting.

6 Incorrect: The guide *doesn't/does not* look well today.
7 Correct
8 Incorrect: Wait a second, Andrew. I'*ll come/I'm coming* with you.
9 Incorrect: Why *aren't you* coming to see the lions?
10 Incorrect: The elephant and its baby *are* coming.
11 Incorrect: Here *comes* the keeper.
12 Incorrect: The cartoonist comes from Germany.
13 Incorrect: Why *do* they throw their scraps on the floor of the cage?
14 Incorrect: *Aren't* I working in the wrong place?

# 1.2 Mini-contexts

| | |
|---|---|
| VERB FORM | Present simple |
| AIM | Presentation of uses of the present simple |
| LEVEL | Intermediate to upper-intermediate |
| TIME | 40 minutes (plus 30 minutes homework) |
| MATERIALS | One copy of 'Mini-contexts' and 'Summary table' for each student (pages 84–5 and 86) |

IN CLASS

## A Reading contexts and answering questions

1 Give each student a copy of 'Mini-contexts'.

2 Ask the class to work individually to read the contexts and complete the tasks.

3 When they have finished, they compare answers with a partner.

4 Go over the answers with the class.

## B Summarising uses and time references

(Note: By 'General time' we mean that it refers to past, present and future, e.g. functions 1 to 5 on the Summary table on p. 14.)

1 Give each student a copy of 'Summary table'.

2 Go over an example of the exercise with the class and ask them to complete it for homework. Students may want to tick columns other than those indicated in the key. This is acceptable if they can argue a strong case, e.g. the future could also be ticked for example sentence 3.

KEY

### A Reading contexts and answering questions: suggested answers

1 a) *What do you* usually *do* at Christmas? b) ii) Christmas holidays in general
2 a) iii) the cassette recorder. b) How do I/you use/record with this cassette recorder?
3 leaves/departs
4 The Earth travels at about 107,000 km an hour.
5 Permanent, hence the present simple. (The present continuous would suggest the situation was temporary.)

6 a) a sports commentator b) the radio/television audience c) He/she is describing the action on the football field for the viewers/listeners.

7 a) a newspaper b) present simple and present continuous c) It is a convention in newspaper headlines to use the present simple for current events. This is space-saving and dramatic. d) present simple and past simple e) It is a convention in newspaper headlines to use the present simple for recent past events. This is space-saving and dramatic.

8 a) ii) the recent past (corresponding to the recency use of the present perfect) b) Yes, the trip is already booked.

9 a) the future b) when, after, once, the moment, the minute, the second c) future simple/future continuous/*going to* d) present simple/present perfect simple

10 a) the joke b) No (there are no past tenses because the joke was fictional and never happened)

11 a) i) Legwork ii) All Our Yesterdays b) The review of the film uses the present simple to describe the plot, which is fictitious. The documentary review uses the past simple because the events actually happened.

B Summary table

| future time clauses | instructions | sports commentary – rapid actions | jokes |

| scientific facts | newspaper headlines: past events | permanent situations |

| habits/routines | fictional plots | reporting verbs: recent past |

| personal timetable/schedule | public timetable/schedule |

| newspaper headlines: present events of short duration |

| Example sentence | General time | Present – at the time of speaking | Past | Future | No time | Use/function |
|---|---|---|---|---|---|---|
| 1 I usually go up to my parents' house. | √ | | | | | habit/routine |
| 2 You press the eject button and then. . . | √ | | | | | instructions |
| 3 There's a slow train that leaves at 10.00. | √ | | | | | public timetable/schedule |
| 4 The Earth travels at about 107,000 km an hour. | √ | | | | | scientific facts |
| 5 Josceline lives in London with her husband. | √ | | | | | permanent situations |
| 6 Baker plays it up the line for Tolmey. | | √ | | | | sports commentary |
| 7 a) Australia mourns | | √ | | | | headlines – present events |

| | | | | | |
|---|---|---|---|---|---|
| b) Two boys die on mountain | | | √ | | headlines – past events |
| 8 a) Peter tells me ... | | | √ | | reporting verbs – recent past |
| b) ... you start your holidays on Saturday. | | | | √ | personal timetable/schedule |
| 9 I'll definitely send one as soon as I arrive. | | | | √ | future time clauses |
| 10 There's this man in a swimming pool and he goes to the top of the diving board. | | | | | √ | jokes |
| 11 Claire becomes involved in murder. | | | | | √ | fictional plots |

The present simple is mainly used to talk about present action in progress at the time of speaking: *False*

# 1.3 Personality

| | |
|---|---|
| VERB FORM | Present simple alongside other tenses |
| AIM | Free practice of the present simple for routine/habit/state in third person singular in an information gap exercise |
| LEVEL | Intermediate to advanced |
| TIME | 50 minutes |
| MATERIALS | One copy of 'Personality Part A' for half of the class (page 87) <br> One copy of 'Personality Part B' for the other half of the class (page 87) |

IN CLASS

## A Previewing the texts

1 Tell the class they are going to read about someone who is well-known in Great Britain.

2 Ask the students to work in pairs to devise questions on what they would like to know about him or her.

3 Write their questions on the board getting students to correct them as necessary.

## B Reading the texts to answer the class's questions

1 Arrange the class in two groups, A and B.

2 Give face down to the students in Group A a copy of 'Personality Part A'. Similarly, give the students in Group B a copy of Part B of the text.

3 Tell the class to scan the text and find the answers to their questions. Students turn over their texts and begin reading.

4 When the time is up, students turn their texts face down and compare answers in their groups. Go over the answers.

## C  Reading for main points

1  Ask the class to read the texts again and to look for the six most important points. Ask them to agree on these points in their groups.

2  Each group should now devise six questions on each of the six main points; these are noted down by the group secretary.

## D  Information exchange

1  Students put away their texts and questions.

2  Each student in Group A pairs off with a student from Group B. They exchange information about the personality.

3  Teacher notes errors during this exchange to correct at the end of the lesson.

## E  Groups exchange questions

The secretary from Group A reads out their six questions for Group B to answer and vice versa.

## F  Deciding the person's identity

1  Write the following possible identities on the board:
Prince Charles
An actor
A pop star
A musician
A racing driver

2  Ask the class to work in groups to decide which identity fits the person in the article.

KEY

An actor, John Nettles.

# 1.4  Galactic shuttle

| | |
|---|---|
| VERB FORM | Present simple |
| AIM | Communicative practice of schedule use of the present simple |
| LEVEL | Intermediate to upper-intermediate |
| TIME | 30 minutes |
| MATERIALS | One copy of 'Planet Planner' for half the class (page 17) |
| | One copy of 'Galaxy Gliders' for a quarter of the class (page 88) |
| | One copy of 'Planet Hoppers' for a quarter of the class (page 89) |

IN CLASS

## A  Previewing the activity

Ask the class to imagine that it is the year 3000 AD and that we can travel through the galaxy. Ask them what information they would like to find out to book an excursion to Saturn.

## B  Assignment of roles

1  Divide the class into 'galactic travellers' and 'galactic travel agents'.

2  Further divide the travel agents into those representing Planet Hoppers and those representing Galaxy Gliders.

3  Assign each pair of travellers a planet and give each traveller a copy of the 'Planet Planner' form.

4  Give each of the travel agents a copy of the appropriate information sheet.

## C  Information seeking/role play

1  Using their 'Planet planner' forms, the travellers go to representatives of both travel agents to find out the necessary information.

2  During the role plays, the teacher can note errors for correction by the students at the end.

3  Finally students come together to decide which travel agent offers the best deal.

# Planet planner

| Name of company | GALAXY GLIDERS | PLANET HOPPERS |
|---|---|---|
| Destination | | |
| Departure time | | |
| Duration of flight | | |
| Price | | |
| Type of service | | |
| Name of craft | | |
| Extra information | | |

# 1.5  Future action

| | |
|---|---|
| VERB FORM | Present simple |
| AIM | Controlled practice of the present simple in future time clauses with a variety of conjunctions |
| LEVEL | Intermediate to upper-intermediate |
| TIME | 30–40 minutes |
| MATERIALS | One copy of 'Future action' for each student (page 90) |

IN CLASS

### A  Checking sequence of tenses

1  Give each student a copy of 'Future action'.

2  Ask students to look at the sentences in the **Take your pick** section. They decide which sentences correctly refer to future action.

### B  Solo/team competition

1  Students can work individually or in teams of two to four, depending on class size.

2  The teacher reads out at random one of the 'Teacher's prompts' from the following list.

**Teacher's Prompts**

| | | |
|---|---|---|
| a) make a cup of tea | f) flood | k) try on |
| b) the fire brigade | g) celebrate | l) runner dead tired |
| c) shops in Palma, the capital | h) cooler | m) take off |
| d) leave you forever | i) sigh with relief | |
| e) arrest him | j) ring | |

3  The students listen and find an appropriate prompt from the 'First future action' column. They select a conjunction, formulate a sentence, and shout 'Future action' as soon as they are ready.

4  The first student to produce an acceptable sentence wins a point for themselves or for the team.
   Example: the teacher reads out *runner dead tired*. The students select *finish the marathon*, and the conjunction *as soon as*. Then they formulate a sentence like, *As soon as the runner finishes the marathon, she'll be dead tired*, and shout 'Future Action'. The teacher writes it on the board.

5  If sentences are not completely correct, they score no points and the next student or team wins a bonus point if they can correct it. Conjunctions can only be used once and the game continues until all the conjunctions have been used up.

VARIATIONS

The teacher can use the same prompts again but insists on a different sentence. The students or teams take turns and have 30 seconds to produce a sentence. Finally, the class can write up sentences from the prompts in the table.

KEY

> ### A  Checking sequence of tenses
>
> a) incorrect b) correct and refers to the future c) incorrect d) correct but refers to habitual action, not future action
> Note: The present perfect simple or continuous are also acceptable in the subordinate clause with future reference. Example: *When she has arrived, she'll send a telegram/As soon as I've been working here for six months, I'll ask for a pay rise.*

# 1.6  We are continuing presently: Part A

| | |
|---|---|
| VERB FORM | Present continuous |
| AIM | Presentation of six uses of the present continuous |
| LEVEL | Intermediate to advanced |
| TIME | 30 minutes |
| MATERIALS | One copy of 'We are continuing presently: Part A' for each student (page 91) |

IN CLASS

### A  Overviewing the contexts

1  Give each student a copy of 'We are continuing presently: Part A'.

2  Ask the students to read through the texts *ignoring the questions* and to categorise them into humorous or cultural.

### B  Reading the contexts and answering the questions

1  Ask the students to work individually on answering the questions and then to compare with a neighbour.

2  Go over the answers with the class.

KEY

> ### B  Answering the questions
>
> 1 a) A pun on *note* which can mean a musical note or a short message. b) yes c) no
> 2 a) No. It's a contradiction for humorous effect. b) at the moment/now/temporarily c) It's seen as temporary. d) Perhaps but this is not certain.
> 3 a) Fewer and fewer. Habits are changing. b) before c) yes d) Only if it is one o'clock on a Sunday!
> 4 a) younger b) future c) yes
> 5 a) No, she sees no reason for pride. She thinks the British are timid. b) A very frequent habit.
> 6 a) past continuous, present continuous b) yes c) The first is from the story, the second from the blurb.

# 1.7 We are continuing presently: Part B

VERB FORM   Present continuous, present simple
AIM   Highlighting and summarising six uses of the present continuous, contrasting present continuous and present simple
LEVEL   Intermediate to advanced
TIME   50 minutes
MATERIALS   One copy of 'We are continuing presently: Part B' for each student (page 92)

IN CLASS

## A Completing the chart

1 Give each student a copy of 'We are continuing presently: Part B'.

2 Ask the class to work individually to enter the uses in the chart and then to compare in pairs. Go over the answers.

## B Timelines option

1 If students are unfamiliar with timelines, give a few examples using the section on Timelines in the Introduction (p. 9).

2 Ask students to draw timelines for each sentence and then to compare with a neighbour. Alternatively, put the timelines in random order on the board for students to match and draw. Go over the answers.

## C Contrasting present continuous and present simple

Students work in pairs to complete the sentences. Go over the answers.

KEY

### A Completing the chart and B Timelines option: suggested answers

| Example sentence | Use | Timeline |
|---|---|---|
| 1 I'm putting out a note for the milkman at the moment. | temporary action in progress now | |
| 2 For the time being I'm spending so much of the day earning money that I don't have time to become rich. | temporary situation | |
| 3 They're usually eating roast beef at one on a Sunday. | regular action around a point of time | |
| 4 I'm having my next birthday when I'm five years older. | future arrangement | |

| 5 English people are always saying sorry. | emphasising very frequent action | PAST        NOW        FUTURE |
| 6 As Ronnie is cleaning his teeth one morning, he sees a message written in the toothpaste | setting the scene: telling a plot | PAST        NOW        FUTURE |

### [C] Contrasting present continuous and present simple

1 a) every day/morning, etc. a) refers to a habit, b) to one particular action
2 a) permanent b) temporary
3 a) one o'clock b) before one
4 a)
5 b)
6 b)

# 1.8  Time box bingo

| | |
|---|---|
| VERB FORM | Present continuous |
| AIM | Sorting time adverbials to correspond to five uses of the present continuous |
| LEVEL | Upper intermediate to advanced |
| TIME | 30 minutes |
| MATERIALS | One copy of 'Time box bingo' for each student (page 93)<br>One copy only of 'Time box bingo' sentences (page 94) |

IN CLASS

### [A] Establishing the time references

1 Give each student a copy of 'Time box bingo'.

2 Working individually, students read the five example sentences and match them to the time boxes (A – E). They compare in pairs and the teacher goes over them.

### [B] Writing in example time adverbials

Students underline the time adverbials in each of the five example sentences and then write them against number 1 in each of the five boxes.

### [C] Playing Bingo

1 One student is given the list of 'Time box bingo sentences'. They read out the first sentence, while the class listens and writes the time adverbial in the correct time box (A – E). If a student is uncertain they can write the adverbial in the 'Not sure' box.

2 The student then hands the list of sentences to the next student who reads out the second sentence, and so on.

3 If a student completes a box with five adverbials, they shout, 'Bingo!'

21

4 The student reads out the five adverbials and the class check they are correct. The teacher intervenes only if necessary.

5 The game then continues.

6 If all twenty sentences have been read and no one has a full box, the class collaborate to sort out the five boxes.

KEY

A Establishing the time references

1 D   2 E   3 C   4 B   5 A

B Writing in example time
adverbials

1 at the moment (Box D)
2 soon (Box E)
3 for the time being (Box C)

4 usually, at 8.30 (Box B)
5 always (Box A)

C Playing Bingo

A 1 (always)
  2 almost always
  3 continually
  4 forever
  5 constantly

B 1 (usually, at 8.30.)
  2 often, at lunchtime
  3 sometimes, at this time of the day
  4 normally, about now
  5 generally, at this time of year

C 1 (for the time being)
  2 nowadays
  3 currently
  4 at present
  5 these days

D 1 (at the moment)
  2 as I stand here
  3 right now
  4 at this very second
  5 at this very moment

E 1 (soon)
  2 tomorrow
  3 at the end of the month
  4 next year
  5 fairly shortly

# 1.9   The changing present

| | |
|---|---|
| VERB FORM | Present continuous |
| AIM | Communicative practice of the present continuous |
| LEVEL | Middle intermediate to advanced |
| TIME | 50 minutes |
| MATERIALS | One copy of 'The changing present' for each student (page 95) |

IN CLASS

A Introducing the topic

Ask students to give examples of things which are changing in the world at the moment. This may result in some initial disagreement and discussion.

### B | Reading and discussing the topics

1  Give each student a copy of 'The changing present' and ask them to read the fourteen statements and to think whether they agree or disagree with them.

2  Arrange the class in groups of two to six and ask them to discuss their views on each of the statements together.

3  During the discussion the teacher can note errors and correct them at the end.

# 1.10  Progress report

| | |
|---|---|
| VERB FORM | Present simple and present continuous |
| AIM | Discrimination between present simple and present continuous |
| LEVEL | Middle intermediate to advanced |
| TIME | 50 minutes (plus optional 50 minute homework) |
| MATERIALS | One copy of 'Progress report' for each student (page 97)<br>For homework, one copy of 'Progress report: Jumble' for each student (page 98) |

IN CLASS

### A | Setting up the activity

1  Arrange the class in pairs and ask each pair to make two large voting sheets – one marked with a large 'A' and one with a large 'B'.

2  The teacher puts up the students' names in pairs on the board and gives each pair a bank of twenty-five points.

### B | Voting for sentences

1  Give each student a copy of 'Progress report'.

2  Using the 'Progress report: Master sheet', the teacher reads out one of the sentences in bold type; these sentences are missing from the students' copies of 'Progress report'.

3  Give the students a short time, say thirty seconds, to decide which of the two sentences (A or B) on their sheet fits.

4  At a given signal, a representative from each pair votes by holding up the prepared sheets with an 'A' or a 'B'.

5  Pairs with the wrong letter displayed lose a point.

6  The teacher gives an explanation for the correct sentence.

VARIATION

As a final written exercise, the students complete their 'Progress report' sheets selecting sentences from the 'Progress report: Jumble' list. This could be done as homework.

# 1.11 Guess who ...

| | |
|---|---|
| VERB FORM | Present simple, present continuous |
| AIM | Communicative practice of the present simple and present continuous |
| LEVEL | Intermediate to upper intermediate |
| TIME | Version 1: 30 minutes    Version 2: 30 minutes    Version 3: 30 minutes |
| MATERIALS | Version 1: One copy of 'Guess who ...' for each student (page 99) |
| | Version 2: One copy of 'Guess who ...' for each group of 2–4 students, cut up into packs of 24 cards |
| | Version 3: Three copies of 'Guess Who ...' for each pair of students, cut up into packs of 24 cards |

VERSION 1
IN CLASS

1 Give each student a copy of 'Guess who ...'.

2 Give an example of how the symbols are used. Example: Ask the class to look at the first picture of Maurice. Either describe the card yourself or elicit possible sentences from the students: *Today he's wearing a suit and tie. He's got a beard. He always travels to work by train and he doesn't usually wear a tie. Today he's going to work by train.*

3 Explain that you will give information about one of the characters and the first student to identify him should raise their hand.

4 When you have practised this exercise a few times, arrange the class in groups of two to four.

5 Now students take turns in their groups to give information about a character while the others listen and try to identify him.

6 Monitor the groups unobtrusively and note down errors for correction at the end.

VERSION 2
IN CLASS

1 As in Version 1, exemplify ways of describing the information on the cards.

2 Arrange the class into groups of two to four students.

3 Place a pack of cards face up in the middle of each group.

4 In turn each student in the group describes one piece of information from the card face up on the top of the pack. Then the top card is put at the bottom of the pack and the new card is described by the group, as before.

5 Monitor the groups and jot down errors for correction at the end.

VERSION 3
IN CLASS

1 As in Version 1, exemplify ways of describing the information on the cards.

2 Arrange the class in pairs and give each pair three packs of cards.

3 Each student takes a pack and lays down the cards face up in front of them.

4 The third pack is put to one side in a stack face down. Each student takes a card from this pack and keeps it confidential.

5 The aim of the game is for each student to identify the card held by the other.

6 In turn each student asks the other a question to which the answer may be only *Yes, No,* or *I don't know.* Example: *Is he wearing a tie?, Does he go to work by train?, Is he travelling to work by train today?*
Through asking questions in this way, each student can eliminate some of the cards and turn them face down until they think that they can identify the card held by their partner.

7 The game can be played several times in this way. A variation is for each student to take two cards from the face down pack for identification by their partner.

8 Monitor unobtrusively and note errors for correction later.


# 1.12  **Perfect choice**

VERB FORM    Present perfect simple and continuous
AIM    Highlighting form of present perfect simple and continuous, correcting errors of form and use in present perfect simple and continuous
LEVEL    Intermediate to advanced
TIME    40 minutes
MATERIALS    One copy of 'Perfect choice' for each student (page 100)


IN CLASS

A  **Previewing the text**

Give the class three clues on the board – *telephone box, $500,000, arrest.*
Students ask the teacher *yes/no* questions to work out the story in the article.

B  **Reading the text**

1 Give each student a copy of 'Perfect choice'.

2 Ask students to read the article and to find out extra details about the story not yet discovered.

C  **Deciding which sentences are grammatically correct**

1 Divide the class into teams of between two and four.

2 Ask the teams to decide which sentences are grammatically correct and which are grammatically incorrect.

D  **Team decision and correction**

1 Each team takes a turn to pick a sentence and say whether it is grammatically correct or not. They receive a point for the right decision.

2 If the team identifies an incorrect sentence, they win a point if they can correct it. If they cannot, the turn passes to the next team and so on.

3 When all the sentences have been discussed, the class write up the correct sentences.

## E Completing substitution table

Ask students to complete the substitution table as a final summary of the form of the present perfect simple and continuous.

KEY

### D Team decision and correction

1  This is about the phone box mystery that *has* at last been solved.
2  'The thief has just stolen from a coin box and *has* just gone.'
3  The FBI *have* been looking for the thief for the last eight years.
4  correct
5  They've just *arrested* the thief.
6  He's been a pain in our phone *for* a long time.
7  Has *James Clark* been charged?
8  correct
9  The FBI have *been* waiting many years for this moment.
10  He's *been* with the police since last week.
11  correct
12  Clark has been *giving* the telephone companies a lot of trouble
13  correct
14  He *was* arrested last week.
15  He's been stealing from phones *for* eight years.
16  correct

### E Substitution table

| Positive | I, you, we, they | (long form) *have* | Present Perfect Active stop*ped* Clark |
| | | (contraction) *'ve* | |
| | He, she, (it) | (long form) *has* | |
| | | (contraction) *'s* | |
| Positive question | *Have* | (I), you, we, they | Present Perfect Passive *been* arres*ted* |
| | *Has* | he, she, it | |
| Negative | I, you, we, they | (long form) *have not* | Present Perfect Continuous *been* steal*ing* again |
| | | (contraction) *haven't* | |
| | He, she, (it) | (long form) *has not* | |
| | | (contraction) *hasn't* | |
| Negative question | (contraction) *Haven't* | (I), you, we, they | |
| | (contraction) *Hasn't* | he, she, it | |
| Tag question | They | (contraction) *'ve* | charg*ed* Clark   *haven't they?* |
| | He | (contraction) *'s* | *hasn't he?* |

# 1.13 Africa braces itself

| | |
|---|---|
| VERB FORM | Present perfect simple |
| AIM | Presentation of present perfect simple with five uses |
| LEVEL | Upper-intermediate to advanced |
| TIME | 30 minutes |
| MATERIALS | One copy of 'Africa braces itself' for each student (page 101) |

IN CLASS

## A Previewing the text

1 Tell the class they are going to read about a natural disaster involving insects.

2 Ask students to work in pairs to write two questions they would like to ask about the text.

3 Write a selection of the students' questions on the board.

4 Pre-teach any necessary vocabulary, e.g. *trigger, menace, plague, swarm.*

## B Reading the text

1 Give each student a copy of 'Africa braces itself' and ask them to find the answers to the questions on the board from the text.

2 Go over the answers.

## C Focusing on time reference

1 Ask the students to underline all the examples of the present perfect simple in the text. Check these with the class.

2 Students now answer questions 1–5. Ensure that the students are aware that the questions refer to the sentences with the present perfect immediately adjacent.

3 Get the class to compare answers in pairs or small groups and then go over the answers.

KEY

## C Focusing on time reference

1 a) recent  b) recently  
2 a) possibly, but it's unlikely  
3 a) we don't know – the indefinite past  
4 a) future  b) yes, in two months' time  
5 a) future  b) no

# 1.14 Locusts past and present

**1.13 'Africa braces itself'** should be completed before this exercise.

| | |
|---|---|
| VERB FORM | Present perfect simple |
| AIM | Highlighting and summarising five uses of the present perfect simple, contrasting the present perfect simple and the past simple, contrasting the present perfect simple and the present simple for future time |
| LEVEL | Middle-intermediate to advanced |
| TIME | 30 minutes |
| MATERIALS | One copy of 'Locusts past and present' for each student (page 102) |

IN CLASS

## A  Completing the chart

Give each student a copy of 'Locusts past and present' and ask them to work individually to enter the uses in the chart. They can then compare with a neighbour before the teacher goes over the answers.

## B  Timelines option

1 If the students are unfamiliar with timelines, give a few examples using the section on Timelines in the Introduction (p. 9).

2 Students draw timelines for each sentence and then compare with a partner. Alternatively, put the timelines in random order on the board for students to match and draw in. Go over the answers.

## C  Contrasting present perfect simple with past simple and present simple

Students work in pairs to contrast the sets of sentences. Work through the answers with the class.

KEY

### A  Completing the chart and  B  Timelines option

| Example sentence | Use | Timeline |
|---|---|---|
| 1 The rains have just brought hope to the starving in Africa. | recent action | PAST    NOW    FUTURE<br>×\| |
| 2 Giant swarms of locusts have been reported in Cape Verde. | indefinite past | PAST    NOW    FUTURE<br>?<br>×\| |
| 3 Experts who have been with the FAO in Mali for years were amazed by the size of one swarm. | past-present period: unfinished | PAST    NOW    FUTURE<br>- - - \| |

| 4 Other countries are waiting until international meetings have been held in two months time. | definite future period | PAST    NOW    FUTURE<br>2 MONTHS<br>├─────────┼────×──── |
| 5 Governments cannot wait until locust swarms have eaten their crops. | indefinite future period | PAST    NOW    FUTURE<br>?<br>├─────────┼─────×─── |

## C  Contrasting present perfect simple with past simple and present simple

1 a) recently  b) merely/only/simply       4 a) over  b) begin
2 b)                                        5 true; a) emphasises the completion
3 a) still working  b) no longer working       of the event

# 1.15  Tense moments

| | |
|---|---|
| VERB FORM | Present perfect simple, past simple |
| AIM | Contrasting the use of the same time adverbials with the present perfect simple and the past simple |
| LEVEL | Intermediate to advanced |
| TIME | 20 minutes |
| MATERIALS | One copy of 'Tense moments' for each student (page 103) |

IN CLASS

## A  Pre-teaching

Pre-teach any necessary vocabulary, e.g. *Christmas pudding, custard, roast beef and Yorkshire pudding, mincemeat, stew, brew, Darjeeling.*

## B  Focusing on the two tenses

Give a copy of 'Tense moments' to each student and ask them to work through 1–9 answering the questions. They can work individually and then compare answers. Go over the answers.

## C  Summarising the time adverbials

1 Ask students to extract the time adverbials from the nine sets of sentences and to enter them in the box.

2 Ask the class to answer the *True/False* question.

KEY

## B  Focusing on the two tenses

1 a) one or more Fridays at an indefinite time in the past b) last Friday

2 a) one or more Christmases at an indefinite time in the past b) last Christmas c) Christmases in general during the speaker's childhood

3  a) can start a conversation
4  a) a live TV programme with a cook
   b) the youth of a famous cook
5  a) logically follows
6  a) a very short time after Christmas
   b) during Christmas

7  a) three hours ago b) more than three
   hours ago
8  a) she is dead b) she is alive
9  a)

## C  Summarising the time adverbials

1  on + time reference
2  at + time reference
3  ever
4  never
5  already

6  this + time reference
7  for + period
8  during + period
9  no time expression

True

# 1.16  Is the time up?

| | |
|---|---|
| VERB FORM | Present perfect simple, past simple |
| AIM | Discrimination between present perfect simple and past simple for finished and unfinished periods (*I didn't see him this morning/I haven't seen him this morning*) |
| LEVEL | Intermediate to advanced |
| TIME | 45 minutes |
| MATERIALS | When photocopying 'Is the time up?' (page 104), mask the right hand side of the page (i.e. the B responses) and make one copy for each student. Then mask the left hand side and make *one copy only* of the B responses. Now cut up the B responses into eighteen sentences. |

IN CLASS

## A  Matching sentences in pairs

1  Divide the class into pairs.

2  Give each student a copy of 'Is the time up?' and distribute the eighteen B responses amongst the pairs as equally as possible.

3  In pairs students match the B responses they have to the appropriate A sentences. The teacher monitors for correctness and the students write the B sentences onto their sheets.

## B  Whole class matches remaining B responses

1  In turn a student from each pair reads out a B response to the class.

2  When the first B response is read out, the other pairs pencil in a '1' after what they consider to be the appropriate sentence. The second B response read out becomes '2' and is likewise entered in after a sentence. This continues until all eighteen have been read out.

3  Once again the first B response is read out and the class decides as a whole which A sentence it corresponds to. They then write the B response in accordingly. This continues until all eighteen responses have been written in.

# 1.17  Have you got the right time?

| | |
|---|---|
| VERB FORM | Present perfect simple, past simple |
| AIM | Matching time adverbials with the present perfect simple and past simple |
| LEVEL | Intermediate to advanced |
| TIME | 20 minutes |
| MATERIALS | One copy of 'Have you got the right time?' for each student (page 105) |

IN CLASS

### A  Matching time adverbials to definitions

Ask the class to work in pairs and to match the first eight time adverbials with the definitions. Go over them with the class.

### B  Matching time adverbials with tenses

1  Ask the class to complete the gaps at the head of the two columns with the tenses which best fit the definitions.

2  Working in pairs students write in the appropriate time adverbials from the box in the two columns.

### C  Time adverbials in context

1  The students write down the two box headings on a separate piece of paper.

2  They work in pairs to produce a sentence for each time adverbial, e.g.

| *Time adverbials connected with past and present* | *Time adverbials connected with past only* |
|---|---|
| I haven't seen anything until now. | He destroyed the plans yesterday |

### D  Answering True/False question

As a review students answer the True/False question at the end of the worksheet.

KEY

### A  Matching time adverbials to definitions

1e 2f 3g 4h 5b 6a 7c 8d
(Note: *so far/up to now* can only be used for actions which can be repeated, e.g. *I've seen the film once so far* (implying there is time to see it again) but *I've seen the film so far* is not acceptable unless it implies *but not the book*)

### B  Matching time adverbials with tenses

1  Time adverbials connected with past and present: Present Perfect Simple
Time adverbials connected with past only: Past Simple

2 Time adverbials connected with past and present:
   until now     ever since     just (= recency)     yet     lately     so far/up to now
   before now     since (+ a period)
   Time adverbials connected with past only:
   yesterday     period (+ ago)     ever after     until (+ past point)     that (+ time)
   last (+ time)     when/before/after (+ past event/state/time)     the other day

D Answering True/False question
   False

# 1.18  Time sort dominoes and A perfect match

| | |
|---|---|
| VERB FORM | Present perfect simple, past simple |
| AIM | Matching adverbials of time to the present perfect or past simple |
| LEVEL | Intermediate to advanced |
| TIME | 40 minutes |
| MATERIALS | One cut-up set of 'Time sort dominoes' for each group of three to five students (page 106) |
| | One copy of 'A perfect match' (page 107) for each student. |

IN CLASS

## A Explaining the rules

1 Arrange the class in groups of three to five working around a table.

2 Explain the rules: the eighteen dominoes are shuffled and dealt to the players in each group, each player receiving six dominoes in a group of three, and different numbers of dominoes in groups of four or five. The first player lays one domino face up in the centre of the table. The player to their left lays a domino from their hand matching a sentence to an adverbial which fits grammatically and logically to the satisfaction of the group. If they cannot lay an appropriate domino, play passes to the next student. Play continues until as many dominoes as possible have been laid.

Point out that *just* is to be used with the meaning of 'recency' and not with the meaning of 'simply' as in *She just stayed in bed.*

## B Playing the game

1 Give the groups sets of dominoes and play begins.

2 When a group finishes, check that the matchings are correct. They can then check other groups' combinations to see if they agree.

## C A perfect match

1 Give each student a copy of 'A perfect match'.

2 Working individually, they check the adverbials A–S against each of the seven sentences and insert the appropriate letters in the boxes. The matchings must be both grammatically and logically correct.

3 Students compare answers in pairs and the teacher goes over the answers.

KEY

[C] **A perfect match**

1 BDKMNPR
2 ACIJLOS
3 ABCEHIJLOS
4 BMNP

5 BDFGKMNPQR
6 ABHI (CEJOS are possible and would needed justifying by the students with appropriate contexts.)
7 BFN

# 1.19  Townscapes

| | |
|---|---|
| VERB FORM | Present perfect simple |
| AIM | Communicative practice of present perfect simple active and/or passive |
| LEVEL | Intermediate to advanced |
| TIME | 30 minutes |
| MATERIALS | One copy of 'Townscapes' for each student (page 108). |

Cut the copies of 'Townscapes' into three parts; the first part should include Camford 1986 and Camford Now, the second part will have Oxtown 1985, and the third part Oxtown Now.

IN CLASS

[A]  **Comparing Camford 1986 and Now**

1  Give each student a copy of Camford 1986 and Camford Now.

2  Ask the class to describe Camford as it was in 1986.

3  Ask students to look at the townscape of Camford Now and describe what has happened. Example: *The factory has been extended.* Check the concept of the indefinite past use of the present perfect by asking questions like, *Do we know when the factory was extended?*

[B]  **Information gap activity**

1  Arrange the class in two groups. Give the students in one group copies of Oxtown 1985 and copies of Oxtown Now to the other group.

2  Tell the first group that they used to live in Oxtown in 1985 but do not live there any more. Ask them to work together to describe the townscape as it was.

3  Tell the second group that they live in Oxtown now and ask them to work together to describe the townscape as it is now.

4  Pair the students off from the two groups so that a resident of Oxtown 1985 works with a resident of Oxtown Now.

5  Ask the residents of Oxtown 1985 to find out what has changed since they lived there. Example: *Is the church still there?/What is the ... like? It's been demolished.* One possibility is to get the past residents to draw the townscape as it is now and the current residents to draw it as it was in 1985.

6  Finally the students return to their original groups and summarise what they have found out.

# 1.20  The search continues

VERB FORM  Present perfect continuous
AIM  Presentation of present perfect continuous with four time references
LEVEL  Intermediate to advanced
TIME  25 minutes
MATERIALS  One copy of 'The search continues' for each student (page 109)

IN CLASS

## A  Writing captions to the cartoon

1  Give each student a copy of the cartoon from 'The search continues' detached from the text.

2  Ask students to write a humorous caption to the cartoon. (An alternative to preview later discussion is to ask them to use the present perfect continuous in the caption).

3  Get students to work in groups to pool their ideas.

4  Write up a selection of the captions volunteered and look at them with the class, making corrections as necessary.

5  Give the students the rest of the sheet and ask the class to read the captions 1 to 4 to the cartoon in the exercise.

## B  Focusing on time references

1  Students underline all the examples of the present perfect continuous in the captions 1 to 4 on the worksheet. Check the class has identified them all.

2  Ask the students to work individually to answer the sets of questions below each of the captions and the *True/False* questions in 5. They then compare their answers.

3  Discuss the answers with the class.

KEY

### B  Focusing on time references

1 a) in the recent past b) no c) yes
d) twenty years ago e) yes f) no
2 a) recently b) yes – the awful smell
c) yes d) process extended in time

3 a) thirty years ago b) yes c) temporary
4 the future
5 a) True b) True c) True d) True

# 1.21   The search has been going on and on and on . . .

**1.20   The search continues** should be completed before this exercise.

| | |
|---|---|
| VERB FORM | Present perfect simple and continuous |
| AIM | Contrasting the present perfect simple and present perfect continuous |
| LEVEL | Intermediate to advanced |
| TIME | 30 minutes |
| MATERIALS | One copy of 'The search has been going on and on and on . . .' for each student (page 110) |

IN CLASS

### A   Contrasting present perfect simple and continuous

1   Give each student a copy of 'The search has been going on and on and on . . .' and ask them to work individually to answer the questions on the contrasting pairs of sentences. These sentences correspond to the captions in 1.20 'The search continues'. They then compare answers in pairs.

2   Discuss the answers with the class.

### B   Checking the grammar summary

Refer the class to the 'Grammar summary: Present perfect simple or present perfect continuous?' Ask the class to work individually to read through it to see if it correlates with the contrastive exercise just completed. The summary is intended to be valid but this is an opportunity for students to raise any questions.

KEY

> ### A   Contrasting present perfect simple and continuous
>
> 1 i) no ii) yes 2) i) true ii) in the first sentence of each pair 3) present perfect simple

# 1.22   Time for a change

| | |
|---|---|
| VERB FORM | Present perfect simple, present perfect continuous |
| AIM | Controlled practice of the present perfect simple and continuous |
| LEVEL | Intermediate to advanced |
| TIME | 20–30 minutes |
| MATERIALS | None |

IN CLASS

### Stimulus to creative response

1   Organise the class into teams of two to four.

2   Explain that you will read out a sentence and that the first student in the first

team has fifteen seconds to respond using the present perfect *continuous*. If the sentence is incorrect, the second student in the first team has a turn to respond to the same prompt and so on. If the sentence is correct, a point is awarded. A new prompt is read by the teacher for the next student. This time the student must offer a sentence in the present perfect *simple*. In this way, each time a correct sentence is offered, the tense changes to the simple or the continuous.
Example: TEACHER: You look tired!
        STUDENT A: Yes, I've been going to bed late all week.
        TEACHER: The grass is wet.
        STUDENT B: I think it's been raining.
The last sentence cannot be accepted as the previous one was also in the continuous.

3 The teacher can use the same prompts more than once but the students' sentences must be different from any before.

### Prompts

a) You look tired.
b) The grass is wet.
c) Your eyes are red.
d) We'll soon arrive at Kennedy Airport.
e) You look thinner.
f) There's milk on the floor.
g) I'm talking to you!
h) I've written to you three times now.
i) I like tennis.
j) You stole my watch.
k) Why didn't you come yesterday?
l) What did you have for lunch yesterday?
m) What are you doing with that jam jar?
n) Why didn't you phone last Sunday?
o) I don't think you know how to play cricket.
p) Didn't you use to go to the cinema a lot?

# 1.23 Cassette sales

| | |
|---|---|
| VERB FORM | Present perfect simple, present perfect continuous, present continuous, past simple |
| AIM | Practice of the above in one context |
| LEVEL | Intermediate to advanced |
| TIME | 40 minutes |
| MATERIALS | One copy of 'Cassette sales' for each student (page 111). One copy of 'Trends in cassette sales', cut up into the twelve sentences (page 112) |

IN CLASS

### A Pre-teaching

1 As an option, pre-teach *rise, fall, increase, decrease, go up, go down, remain stable, sharp(ly), slight(ly), dramatic(ally), fluctuate, consistent(ly)*

### B Exemplifying the listening/reading task

1 Give each student a copy of the 'Cassette sales' graphs.

2 Tell the class you will describe one of the graphs and they must identify it.

3 Describe one of the graphs for identification. Example: *Sales of cassettes have remained at the same level for the last six years.* This matches graph number 7.

### C Reading/listening task

1 Give one sentence each from 'Trends in cassette sales' to twelve students.

2 In turn the students with sentences read them out and the rest of the class work individually to identify the graph they are describing and mark them with letters a) – 1).

3 The students now read their sentences again and the class agree on the graph described in each case. Once agreement has been made, the student dictates the sentence for the rest of the class to write under the appropriate graph, or, for advanced classes, students describe the graph themselves.

KEY.

### C Reading/Listening task

1 d)  2 e)  3 h)  4 j)  5 a)  6 k)  7 b)  8 l)  9 f)  10 g)  11 i)  12 c)

# 1.24 Ups and downs

**1.23 'Cassette sales'** should be completed before this exercise.

| | |
|---|---|
| VERB FORM | Present perfect simple, present perfect continuous, present continuous, past simple |
| AIM | Discrimination between and communicative use of present perfect, present continuous, and past simple |
| LEVEL | Intermediate to advanced |
| TIME | 45 minutes |
| MATERIALS | One copy of 'Ups and downs: Part A' for half of the class and one copy of 'Ups and downs: Part B' for the other half of the class (Page 113) |

IN CLASS

### A Exemplifying the task

1 Put an example of the activity on the board.
Example:

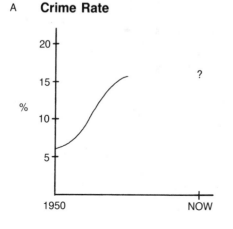

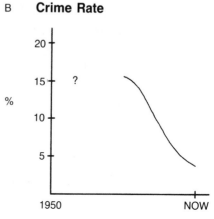

37

2  Ask the class what questions they could ask to get the missing information.
Example: *What happened to the crime rate after about 1970?*

3  Ask the class to describe the missing information.
Example: *The crime rate has been falling since then and is continuing to fall at the moment.*

### B  Completing the graphs and information gap

1  Arrange the class in pairs.

2  Give one student in each pair a copy of 'Ups and downs: Part A' and the other student a copy of 'Ups and downs: Part B'.

3  Pairs complete the plots on their graphs by exchanging information.

4  One possibility at the information exchange stage is to insist that the students use the present perfect whenever possible.

### C  Summarising the information in the graphs

1  The pairs now collaborate to construct a sentence for their graph which includes the present perfect.

2  Collate possible sentences from the class on the board.

### D  Comparison of trends in other countries

The class discuss how the trends in the graph compare in their opinion with the situation in their own country. This can be done in groups and then as a class.

# 1.25  Deleted transformations

| | |
|---|---|
| VERB FORM | Present perfect simple and present perfect continuous |
| AIM | Controlled practice of the present perfect, transforming sentences into the present perfect |
| LEVEL | Intermediate to advanced |
| TIME | 40 minutes |
| MATERIALS | One copy of 'Deleted transformations' for each student (page 114) |

IN CLASS

### A  Setting up the game

1  Arrange the class into groups of two to four students.

2  Put an example of the exercise on the board:
Charlie went to the Pyramids only yesterday.
___        has        ___   ___   ___   ___   ___ .
  1      2      3      4      5      6      7
Explain that the students have to fill the gaps to make a sentence which means the same as the first sentence. The students can ask the teacher questions about the gaps to which the answers are *yes* and *no*, for example, *Is the sixth word 'Pyramids'?* Do the example on the board with the class.

### B  Playing the game

1  Give each student a copy of 'Deleted transformations'.

2 Explain that each team in turn has fifteen seconds to ask only one *yes/no* question. If the teacher answers *yes*, the team gains a point. Keep a running total of the points for each team on the board.

VARIATION

Instead of teams asking questions in turn, a team representative asks a question at any time, but no points are scored for correct guesses. Instead the winning team is the first to fill all the gaps.

KEY

A Setting up the game

| Charlie | has | just | gone | to | the | Pyramids. |
|---------|-----|------|------|----|-----|-----------|
| 1 | 2 | 3 | 4 | 5 | 6 | 7 |

B Playing the game

1 [1]He [2]has [3]not [4]come [5]upstairs [6]yet.
2 [1]Jean [2]has [3]just [4]set [5]off [6]for [7]Liverpool.
3 [1]This [2]is [3]the [4]first [5]time [6]she [7]has [8]eaten [9]roast [10]beef.
4 [1]We [2]have [3]not [4]been [5]to [6]the [7]wax [8]museum [9]for [10]ages.
5 [1]Have [2]you [3]ever [4]needed [5]glasses [6]before?
6 [1]They [2]have [3]not [4]been [5]swimming [6]since [7]the [8]beginning [9]of [10]autumn.
7 [1]I [2]have [3]been [4]waiting [5]for [6]my [7]wife [8]for [9]an [10]hour.
8 [1]Nobody [2]has [3]written [4]to [5]me [6]yet.
9 [1]It [2]is [3]ages [4]since [5]we [6]had [7]a [8]thunderstorm.
10 [1]They [2]have [3]been [4]going [5]to [6]Hong [7]Kong [8]for [9]three [10]years.

# 1.26 Deadly mistake

| | |
|---|---|
| VERB FORM | Present simple, present continuous, present perfect simple, present perfect continuous |
| AIM | Identifying the correct uses of the four present tenses |
| LEVEL | Intermediate to advanced |
| TIME | 45 minutes |
| MATERIALS | One copy of 'Deadly mistake' for each student (page 115) |

IN CLASS

A Teams correct and select

1 Arrange students in groups of two to four.

2 Give each student a copy of 'Deadly mistake'.

3 Ask the teams to decide which sentences contain errors and which of the options, where relevant, are correct.

B Team competition

1 Each team takes a turn to select a speech bubble and correct the error of use or select the correct option.

2  They receive a point for correction or right selection. If they make a mistake the turn passes to the next team.

KEY

## B  Team competition

1  The body *has been* here for three hours.
2  Correct.
3  You can't go inside – they *are taking* photographs now.
4  It's a long time *since we had/since we've had* a murder like this.
5  He's *argued* with his wife before.
6  Somebody *came* earlier but nobody was at home.
7  This is the first time I *have seen* so much blood.
8  I *found* the corpse at five a.m.
   That's nothing unusual. I *have often found* corpses at that time.
9  The photographer *hasn't taken* any photos yet.
10  Yes, he *cut* himself (+ a time expression, e.g. *when he was a child*).
11  But *I'm not going* near it.
12  *I checked* the fingerprints with our records immediately after I *took* them.
13  Yes, he's *been* on holiday.
14  They have *had* this apartment since 1987.
15  *Nobody* has ever seen such a terrible crime.
16  Are you sure the body has been here *for* three hours?
17  Correct.
18  *Did he lose* a lot of blood?
19  ... I want some money for that vase you *broke*.
20  *Have you ever used* one?

# Section 2

# Pasts

## 2.1 Fruit machine

| | |
|---|---|
| VERB FORM | Past simple |
| AIM | Correcting errors of form |
| LEVEL | Intermediate to upper-intermediate |
| TIME | 50 minutes |
| MATERIALS | One copy of 'Fruit machine' for each student (page 116) |

IN CLASS

### A  Groups decide on scoring combinations

1  Explain that the 'Fruit machine' contains eighteen pairs of sentences. Some pairs consist of two correct sentences, some consist of two incorrect sentences, some consist of a correct and an incorrect sentence. Emphasise that incorrect or correct refers to grammatical form and not factual content.

2  Put students into groups of two to four. Give each student a copy of 'Fruit machine'. Give the class about twenty minutes working in groups to identify combinations of correct/correct, incorrect/incorrect, correct/incorrect and incorrect/correct pairs of sentences.

### B  Group competition

1  Explain the scoring system. Groups score one point for identifying an appropriate combination and a further point if they can make any necessary corrections. If they are successful, they may have up to two more turns. If they are successful on three consecutive turns, they hit the Jackpot and receive an extra two bonus points.
   If they cannot make the corrections, the turn passes to the next team who win the point for correction if they can and then also have their own turn.
(Note: The pairs of sentences become progressively more difficult and the teacher may wish to select a cut-off point beyond which a class at a lower level need not go.)

KEY

1  Incorrect/incorrect
   London's population *did not increase* from 1955 to 1988.
   The population *did not increase*.
2  Correct/correct
3  Incorrect/incorrect
   In the 1900 Olympics Alvin Kraenzlein *came* first in four athletics events.
   He *came* first in four events.
4  Incorrect/incorrect
   She didn't *like* it.
   She didn't *like* it.

5 Incorrect/incorrect
Why did they *buy* it?
Why *did* they *buy* it?
6 Incorrect/incorrect
He *fell* down the stairs two minutes ago.
He *fell* down the stairs two minutes ago.
7 Incorrect/correct
She *felt* happy yesterday.
8 Incorrect/correct
The English football team, Nottingham Forest, once *won* forty-two matches in a row.
9 Incorrect/correct
Who *told you*?/Who *did you tell*?
10 Correct/incorrect
He ate it in 1983, *didn't he*?
11 Correct/correct
*You did this*? spoken with a rising intonation in surprise.
12 Correct/incorrect
*dreamed* and *dreamt* are both acceptable.
A Norwegian *lay* on a bed of nails for 274 hours in 1984.
13 Correct/correct
14 Correct/correct
*did* used for emphasis and stressed
15 Correct/correct
*Did I not*, the uncontracted form for emphasis.
16 Correct/incorrect
He didn't know why *they didn't* come.
17 Correct/incorrect
In Toronto, Terry McGaurant *preferred* to ride his motorbike solo up the 1760 steps of the 550 metre high Canadian National Tower.
18 Correct/incorrect
Alaska State Museum once *paid* £34,750 for a hat.

# 2.2 Past a joke

VERB FORM  Past simple
AIM  Presentation of the past simple
LEVEL  Intermediate to advanced
TIME  20–30 minutes
MATERIALS  One copy of 'Past a joke' for each student (pages 117–18)

IN CLASS

## A Reading the contexts and answering the questions

1 Give each student a copy of 'Past a joke' and ask them to work alone reading the texts and answering the questions on each text. Tell them the first two stories are true.

2 Ask students to compare answers and finally go over them with the class.

## B Completing the summary of past simple uses

1 Ask students to work individually and to circle either *True* or *False* for each of

the summary statements on uses of the past simple. For help they should refer to the texts they have read.

2 Finally ask them to compare summaries and then go over the answers with the whole class.

KEY

> ### A Reading the contexts and answering the questions
>
> 1 a) several actions  b) one action  c) complete
> 2 a) at the same time b) one after the other
> 3 a) the present  b) Could you help me? I wonder if you could help me ... I wondered if you could help me ...
> 4 a) I would  b) future  c) a preference  d) sooner
> 5 a) two  b) yes  c) the present
> 6 a) the present  b) no  c) It intensifies the meaning of sentences, but can be omitted.
>
> ### B Completing the summary of past simple uses
>
> All of the statements are **True**! This provides the students with a concise summary of uses.

# 2.3 Tunnel ball

| | |
|---|---|
| VERB FORM | Principal parts of irregular verbs – infinitive, past simple, past participle |
| AIM | Review of principle parts of irregular verbs |
| LEVEL | Intermediate to upper-intermediate |
| TIME | 20 minutes |
| MATERIALS | For the teacher, infinitives of a minimum of ten irregular verbs on large pieces of paper or flashcards |

IN CLASS

## A Arranging groups

1 Divide the class into groups of six to twelve students.

2 Arrange the groups in columns facing the board.

3 Give the student at the front of each column a board marker.

4 The teacher stands at the back of the columns and asks the student at the back of each column to turn and face them.

## B Playing tunnel ball

1 The teacher holds up a paper or flashcard with an infinitive, e.g. COME.

2 The student at the back of each column whispers the verb to the next student in the column who must work out and pass on the *infinitive, past simple* and *past participle* of the verb, if they know them (e.g. COME, CAME, COME), to the next student. If they do not know them they just pass on the infinitive.

43

3 The next student either passes on the infinitive or the complete sequence (COME, CAME, COME) to the student in front of them and so on, until the student at the front of the column writes them up on the board.

4 The 'Tunnel ball' continues in this way until all of the verbs have been passed down and written up.

5 The teacher awards points for the correct verb forms written up by each team.

# 2.4 Volleyball

| | |
|---|---|
| VERB FORM | Principal parts of irregular verbs – infinitive, past simple, past participle |
| AIM | Memorisation of the principal parts of irregular verbs |
| LEVEL | Intermediate to upper-intermediate |
| TIME | 20–30 minutes |
| MATERIALS | One copy of 'Volleyball' for every four students (page 119). Cut the sets of verbs into strips, one set for each student in the class. |

IN CLASS

## A Setting up 'Volleyball' and explaining the rules

1 Arrange the class into two teams facing each other.

2 Give each student a set of verbs, set A, B, C, or D.

3 Explain that a student from the first team selects a verb from their set and calls it out to the second team. A student in the second team must call back the *past simple*, the first team must then call back the *past participle*. Now a student from the second team selects a verb from their set and calls it out to the first team and so on. A mistake wins a point for the other team.

## B Playing 'Volleyball'

1 The teacher sets either a target number of points to be won or a time limit.

2 The teacher does not give the correct forms when mistakes are made but simply shouts 'Mistake' and adds a point to the running total of the appropriate team on the board. The teacher also makes a list on the board of the infinitives of the verbs which cause mistakes.

3 At the end of the game, each team has a turn to give the principal parts of one of the verbs listed on the board and scores extra points.

4 For subsequent games of 'Volleyball', students should exchange sets of verbs.

## Acknowledgement

This is an extension of 'Grammar tennis' by Mario Rinvolucri in *Grammar Games* (CUP 1984).

# 2.5 Who was Jack the Ripper?

| | |
|---|---|
| VERB FORM | Past continuous |
| AIM | Highlighting the form of the past continuous |
| LEVEL | Intermediate to advanced |
| TIME | 20–30 minutes |
| MATERIALS | One copy of 'Who was Jack the Ripper?' for each student (page 120) |

IN CLASS

## A  Groups locate errors of form

1 Arrange students in groups of two to four and give each student a copy of the worksheet.

2 Elicit an example of the past continuous from the class.

3 Tell the class there are six errors of form (not use) in the past continuous in the text and ask the groups to work together to find them.

## B  Correcting errors

In turn groups receive a point for locating an error and a point for correcting it. If they are unsuccessful in correction, the next team has a chance to gain a bonus point before taking their own turn.

## C  Completing the substitution table

As a summary of the form of the past continuous, students complete the table.

KEY

## B  Correcting errors

line 5: the police *were patrolling* (two errors)
line 7: They *were* examining the body
line 14: some people were *singing* and *dancing*
line 15: *was he* killing
line 21: Were *the police hiding some of the evidence*

## C  Completing the substitution table

PAST CONTINUOUS

| Positive | Last night I *was reading* about Jack the Ripper. On a dark night in 1888 he *was following* Polly Nichols through the streets of London. The police *were patrolling* the streets thirty minutes before the murder. |
|---|---|
| Negative | They *were not looking* for a thief |
| Negative contraction | *weren't* |

| Questions: Positive | Why *were you reading* about Jack the Ripper? |
|---|---|
| Negative | Why *weren't* the police *looking* for a thief? |
| Tag | Jack the Ripper *was killing* for some strange reason, *wasn't he*? |
| Passive | Polly *was being followed* through the London streets. |

# 2.6  Continuous contexts

(After doing this exercise, you should also complete 2.7 'Continuous continued'.)

| | |
|---|---|
| VERB FORM | Past continuous |
| AIM | Presentation of six uses of the past continuous |
| LEVEL | Upper intermediate to advanced |
| TIME | 30 minutes |
| MATERIALS | One copy of 'Continuous contexts' for each student (pages 121–2) |

IN CLASS

## A  Setting up teams and giving instructions

1  Put the students in teams of two to four depending on class size.

2  Give an example of the gapfilling task on the board:

\_\_\_\_ _____ \_\_\_\_ _____   London is Dave's home.
　　1　　　2　　　3　　　　4

Explain that the gapped sentence means the same as the sentence written on the board. Each team takes a turn to guess one word in one gap. For example, if the first team thinks that *He* is in gap 1, they are successful and receive one point. The turn then passes to the next team and so on. Get the class to try the example on the board; the solution is: ¹*He* ²*lives* ³*in* ⁴*London.*
If viable alternatives are offered, then accept them.

## B  Playing the game

1  Elicit an example of the past continuous from the class.

2  Tell the class that the contexts A to F present six different uses of the past continuous. The bold type highlights the particular use focused on.

3  Begin with context A and only go on to context B, when context A is complete. Keep a running total of points for each team on the board.

4  After each round give them the first letter of one of the remaining gaps; if all of

the first letters have been given, give the second letter of one of the words, and so on.

5 Now do the 'Continuous continued' worksheet (2.7) with the class.

KEY

### B Playing the game

A 'Honestly, Constable, I [1]*was* [2]*aiming* at the [3]*fire* alarm when [4]*you* [5]*came* along.'

B [1]*He* [2]*was* always [3]*getting* [4]*divorced* until [5]*he* [6]*met* [7]*his* twenty-second [8]*wife*, Eva.

C '[1]*Excuse* me, Mr Smithers, [2]*I* [3]*was* [4]*wondering* whether [5]*you* [6]*could* [7]*tell* [8]*me* where you put the key to the office tea cupboard.'

D While she [1]*was* [2]*going* [3]*back* [4]*to* [5]*the* department store, [6]*thieves* [7]*were* [8]*burgling* her [9]*house*.

E At three on a summer afternoon Henry Bourse [1]*was* [2]*filming* [3]*underwater* [4]*near* Melbourne. After some time a shark suddenly bit off his leg and swam away with it. Henry continued filming. [5]*His leg* [6]*was* [7]*artificial*. Another shark [8]*had* [9]*bitten* [10]*off* other leg several years earlier.

F In 1947 the crew of the destroyer, HMS Saintes [1]*was* [2]*training* [3]*for* [4]*three* [5]*weeks* [6]*in* Portsmouth. Their task was to fire at a target pulled by the tugboat, Buccaneer. They fired, [7]*missed* the target and [8]*sank* the tugboat!

# 2.7 Continuous continued

**2.6 'Continuous contexts'** should be completed before this exercise.

VERB FORM Past continuous, past simple
AIM Highlighting and summarising six uses of the past continuous, contrasting past simple and past continuous
LEVEL Intermediate to advanced
TIME 30 minutes
MATERIALS One copy of 'Continuous continued' for each student (page 123)

IN CLASS

### A Completing the chart

1 Give each student a copy of 'Continuous continued' and ask them to enter the uses in the chart working individually, and then to compare answers in pairs. Go over them with the class.

### B Timelines option

If students are unfamiliar with timelines, give a few examples using the section on Timelines in the Introduction (p. 9).
Students draw timelines for each sentence. Alternatively, put timelines on the board in random order for the students to match and draw in.

### C Contrasting past continuous and past simple

Students work in pairs to read the six sets of contrasting sentences and to answer the questions

47

KEY

| A | Completing the chart and | B | Timelines option |

| Example sentence | Use | Timeline |
|---|---|---|
| Excuse me, I was wondering whether you could tell me where the key is. | polite, tentative request | PAST NOW FUTURE |
| At three he was filming underwater near Melbourne. | action in progress around a point of time | PAST NOW FUTURE<br>3.00 |
| In 1947 the crew were training for three weeks in Portsmouth. | action in progress for a period | PAST NOW FUTURE<br>3 WEEKS |
| I was aiming at the fire alarm when you came along. | interrupted action | PAST NOW FUTURE |
| He was always getting divorced until he met Eva. | emphasising very frequent action | PAST NOW FUTURE |
| While she was returning to the store, thieves were burgling her house. | simultaneous actions | PAST NOW FUTURE |

C Contrasting past continuous and past simple

1 i) if  ii) b  2 a) before three  b) at three  3 past continuous as in b)  4 a) he was in the process of aiming when the police came along  b) the police arrived and then he aimed  5 a  6 b

# 2.8 Sea saga

| | |
|---|---|
| VERB FORM | Past continuous, past simple |
| AIM | Communicative practice of six uses of the past continuous, contrast between past simple and past continuous |
| LEVEL | Upper-intermediate to advanced |
| TIME | 30–40 minutes |
| MATERIALS | One copy of 'Sea saga: Part A' for half of the students in the class, and one copy of 'Sea saga: Part B' for the other half of the class (pages 124–125) |

IN CLASS

A Pre-teaching

Pre-teach the following items: *deck, bridge, to row, crew, to jam, to drift, lifeboat, railings, cabin.*

## B Grouping the class and setting reading tasks

1 Arrange the class in two groups – A and B.

2 Give each student in Group A a copy of 'Sea saga: Part A' and each student in Group B a copy of 'Sea saga: Part B'.

3 Ask the students to read their texts and, working individually, to number the pictures in the correct order corresponding to the story.

4 Get the students to compare picture sequences with a partner from the same group.

5 Ask students to answer the *True/False* questions and to compare answers with a partner in the same group.

## C Story comparison

1 Pair students off one from Group A and one from Group B.

2 Ask the pairs to work together through their answers to the *True/False* questions. They try to find six differences between the two versions of the story.

3 Go over the differences with the class.

KEY

### B Setting reading tasks

1 m  2 d  3 b  4 h  5 g  6 l  7 k  8 j  9 a  10 c  11 e  12 f  13 i

### B True/False questions

Sea saga: Part A
1 True  2 False  3 True  4 True  5 True
6 True

Sea saga: Part B
1 False  2 True  3 False  4 False
5 False  6 False

### C Story comparison

| *Sea saga: Part A* | *Sea saga: Part B* |
|---|---|
| 1 we were enjoying a four month cruise | We had enjoyed four months of our cruise |
| 2 We were about to cross the Bay of Biscay | we were steaming across the Bay of Biscay |
| 3 I was running upstairs to the next deck when the captain suddenly raced past me | I ran upstairs to the deck where I saw the captain |
| 4 Alarm bells rang and the next minute sailors tried to lower a lifeboat | Alarm bells were ringing and sailors were trying desperately to lower a lifeboat |
| 5 they were always having problems with the boats | they had only had one previous problem with the boats |
| 6 we were wondering whether you could help us with our enquiries | we want to ask you one or two questions |

# 2.9 Assam: Perfect tea

| | |
|---|---|
| VERB FORM | Past perfect simple and past perfect continuous |
| AIM | Highlighting the forms – error correction and completing substitution tables |
| LEVEL | Intermediate to advanced |
| TIME | 40 minutes |
| MATERIALS | One copy of 'Assam: Perfect tea' for each student (page 126) |

IN CLASS

## A Pre-teach vocabulary of tea-making

1 Pre-teach: *stale, brew, tea leaves, tea pot.*

2 Put the following jumbled table on the board:

| | |
|---|---|
| boil | for three to five minutes |
| brew | fresh water |
| put in | the tea pot |
| warm | boiling water |
| pour on | fresh, not stale tea leaves |

3 Ask the students to match the items in the two columns.

4 Students put the instructions for tea-making in the right order.

## B Error correction

Students read the nine sentences, A1 to B5, and correct errors of form, working first individually and then in pairs.

## C Completing the substitution tables

Ask the students to complete the two substitution tables as a final summary of the form of the past perfect simple and continuous.

KEY

### A Vocabulary of tea-making

Boil fresh water. Warm the tea pot. Put in fresh, not stale tea leaves. Pour on the boiling water. Brew for three to five minutes.

### B Error correction

A1 Incorrect
   They had already *thrown* in the tea leaves when they realised I needed warming first.
A2 Incorrect
   Had *you been* expecting the water to be so hot when they poured it in?
A3 Incorrect
   They waited till the tea *had been brewing/had brewed* for ten minutes before somebody poured it out.
A4 Correct
B1 Incorrect
   I had been *asleep/sleeping* for a few minutes before I noticed the hot water pouring in.

B2 Incorrect
Why *had they* forgotten to warm the pot before putting in the tea leaves?
B3 Incorrect
Your tea had been left for too long before they poured it out, *hadn't it*?
B4 Incorrect (but acceptable in some varieties of English)
They *hadn't/had not* put enough leaves in, so the tea was too weak.
B5 Incorrect
Why hadn't the tea *been made* properly?

## C Completing the substitution tables

### Past perfect simple

| | |
|---|---|
| **Positive** | I *had made* the tea before the water was hot enough. |
| **Positive contraction** | *'d* |
| **Negative** | He *had not warmed* the pot before he put in the tea leaves. |
| **Negative contraction** | *hadn't* |
| **Questions:** | |
| **Positive** | Why *had you made* the tea before the water boiled? |
| **Negative** | *hadn't you made* |
| **Tag** | They *had made* the tea before the water boiled, *hadn't they*? |
| **Passive** | The tea *had been made* before the water boiled. |
| **Passive question** | Why *had* the tea *been made* before the water boiled? |

### Past perfect continuous

| | |
|---|---|
| **Positive** | She *had been making* tea for twenty years before Emma told her about warming the pot. |
| **Positive contraction** | *'d* |
| **Negative** | We *had not been making* tea in the afternoon until Emma came to stay. |
| **Negative contraction** | *hadn't* |
| **Questions: Positive** | How long *had you been making* tea before Emma told you about warming the pot? |
| **Negative** | Why *hadn't you been making* tea properly before Emma came to stay? |
| **Tag** | We *had been making* tea for twenty years before Emma told us about warming the pot, *hadn't we*? |

# 2.10 Penalty shot

| | |
|---|---|
| VERB FORM | Past perfect simple, past simple |
| AIM | Presentation of three uses of the past perfect simple, contrast with the past simple |
| LEVEL | Upper-intermediate to advanced |
| TIME | 40 minutes |
| MATERIALS | One copy of 'Penalty shot' Sheets A and B for each student (pages 127–128) |

IN CLASS

## A Reading the text

1 Pre-teach any necessary vocabulary, e.g. *penalty shot, goalkeeper, save a goal, miss a shot.*

2 Give each student a copy of 'Penalty shot: Sheet A' and get them to look only at the cartoon. The copies can be folded to conceal the text. Elicit the story line of the cartoon.

3 Tell students they are going to read a true story and their task is to find differences between the story and the cartoon.

4 Students read the story and discuss the differences.

## B Focusing on time reference

1 Ask students how the past perfect simple is formed and elicit some examples. The students underline all the examples of the past perfect simple in the text. Check these with the class – some students may incorrectly underline the past simple of *have* in *Marie-Jeanne had nothing worse ...* or the past of the modal in *Pierre and the young girl's shocked parents had to wait ...* or *Pierre had to wait ....*

2 Tell the class they are going to answer questions focusing on the use of the past perfect simple and ask them to answer questions 1 to 4. Ask them to compare with a partner and then you can discuss the answers with the whole class.

## C Completing the chart (Sheet A)

Ask the class to complete the chart by entering the three uses of the past perfect simple against the example sentences and then answer the *True/False* question at the end. Discuss the answers with the class.

## D Timelines option

1 If the class is unfamiliar with timelines, give a few examples, using the section on Timelines in the Introduction (p. 9).

2 Students draw timelines for the three sentences containing the past perfect simple which they have underlined in the text. Alternatively, put the timelines on the board in random order for the class to match with the sentences.

## E Comparing past simple and past perfect simple

1 Give each student a copy of 'Penalty Shot: Sheet B'.

2 Ask the class to ring *True, False,* or *No information* for each of the statements 1 to 4.

3  Get them to compare answers in pairs and then you go over the answers.

4  The students then tick or cross the statements a)–c). Get them to work individually and then to compare answers in pairs.

F  **Summary table**

1  Pre-teach the expressions, 'Age before Beauty', 'There is no smoke without fire', and 'A rose by any other name smells as sweet'.

2  Working individually and then in pairs, students complete the chart; they tick or put a cross in the columns against each sentence as appropriate.

3  Go over the answers.

KEY

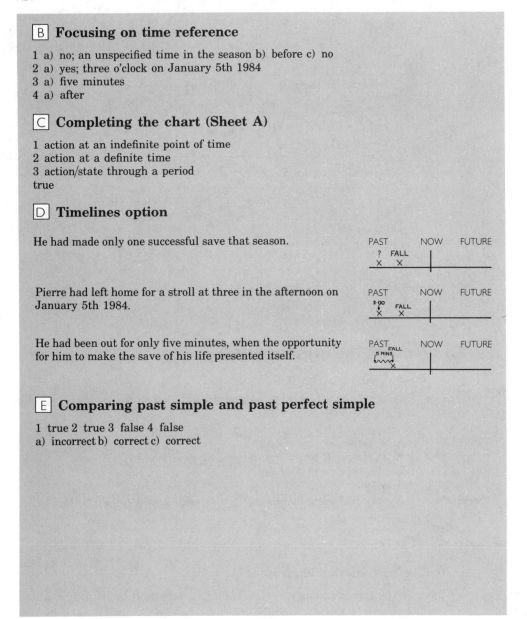

B  **Focusing on time reference**

1  a) no; an unspecified time in the season  b) before  c) no
2  a) yes; three o'clock on January 5th 1984
3  a) five minutes
4  a) after

C  **Completing the chart (Sheet A)**

1  action at an indefinite point of time
2  action at a definite time
3  action/state through a period
true

D  **Timelines option**

He had made only one successful save that season.

Pierre had left home for a stroll at three in the afternoon on January 5th 1984.

He had been out for only five minutes, when the opportunity for him to make the save of his life presented itself.

E  **Comparing past simple and past perfect simple**

1 true 2 true 3 false 4 false
a) incorrect b) correct c) correct

---

F Summary table

'Age before beauty': **Past perfect simple before past simple**
If there are two actions in the past, the past perfect simple can be used for the first action in the sequence.

'There is no smoke without fire': **There is no past perfect simple without a past simple**
When a verb is in the past perfect simple, there will always be another verb linked with it in the past simple in the same time period and in the same text (although not necessarily in the same sentence.)

'A rose by any other name smells as sweet': The past simple can sometimes be used in place of the past perfect simple without a change of meaning

| | | | |
|---|---|---|---|
| Pierre had saved only one goal that season. However, this was soon to change. | × | √ | √ |
| Pierre had left home for a stroll at three . . . . . . he heard screams. | √ | √ | √ |
| Pierre had strolled about for five minutes when he heard screams. | × | √ | √ |
| He had turned the corner when he heard screams. | × | √ | √ |

# 2.11 Romeo, Romeo, ohhh . . .

This activity follows on from the presentation of the past perfect simple in 2.10 'Penalty shot'.

VERB FORM   Past perfect simple
AIM   Written practice of past perfect simple with three uses
LEVEL   Upper-intermediate to advanced
TIME   60 minutes
MATERIALS   One copy of 'Romeo, Romeo ohhh ...' for each student (page 129)

IN CLASS

A Prediction exercise

1 The teacher writes the following key words on the board:
*wedding grass balcony horror*

2  The students try to predict the storyline by asking questions to which the teacher answers *Yes, No, Not important* or *bad grammar*. If the grammar is bad, the question can only be answered if it is rephrased correctly. The activity continues until the students reach a stalemate or predict most of the story.

3  The teacher can note down any errors in the students' questions and go over corrections at the end of the exercise.

### B  Pre-teaching

Pre-teach: *grab, topple, pose, bride, groom.*

### C  Reading and rewriting the text

1  Give each student a copy of 'Romeo, Romeo … ohhh …' and ask them to read it to find any new details which they had not predicted.

2  Refer students to the example sentences of the past perfect simple in 2.10 'Penalty shot'. Ask them to rewrite 'Romeo, Romeo … ohhh …' to incorporate three similar sentences in the past perfect simple without changing the factual details.

3  Students exchange scripts for checking before handing them to the teacher.

VARIATION

Ask the students to rewrite the story from the point of view of the groom when they incorporate the past perfect simple.

KEY

### C  Reading and rewriting the text

There are of course several different ways of rewriting the story – here is just one possibility:

Kenneth Burke had been married once before. He had to wait two years until his new girlfriend, Diana, agreed to be his second wife.

They had been married at eleven and the wedding reception was at twelve in their sixth floor flat in Philadelphia, USA. They were having photographs taken with their guests and went out onto the balcony. They posed for a group photograph and the camera had just flashed when the groom lost his balance. He grabbed hold of his wife and sent them both toppling to the ground below. Their guests watched in horror and had to wait until the couple reached the ground to see that they were both alive. The newlyweds landed on a patch of rain-softened grass and lived. They had been married for two hours and survived!

# 2.12  Flashback

| | |
|---|---|
| VERB FORM | Past perfect simple, past simple |
| AIM | Controlled practice in past perfect simple in sequencing and narrative |
| LEVEL | Intermediate to advanced |
| TIME | 40–50 minutes |
| MATERIALS | One copy of 'Flashback' for each student (page 130) |

IN CLASS

## A Example of Activity: The most unsuccessful escape from prison!

1  Write up the following on the board:
    A dig/tunnel/six months       B send back/jail
    C plan/escape/Saltillo prison D 1975/75 criminals/come out/tunnel/into local
                                      courtroom

2  Tell students that this is a true story which happened in Mexico.

3  Ask students to put the events into the correct sequence and number them 1–4.
    Then get the students to tell the story in the past orally.

4  Now ask the students to retell the story with the events in the following
    sequence: D C A B. They should only use the connectors *but* and *and*.

## B Sequencing and rewriting 'The least alert burglar'.

1  Give each student a copy of 'Flashback'.

2  As in the example exercise, tell students to sequence the parts of the jigsaw of
    this true story and to compare solutions in pairs.

3  Students retell the story in the past orally in its correct chronological sequence.

4  Put the class into three groups – 'Flashback 1', 'Flashback 2' and 'Flashback 3'.
    In their groups, students rewrite the story in the given sequence. They check
    each other's scripts within their groups.

5  Arrange the students in threes, one student from each 'Flashback' group.
    Students swop their scripts for checking.

6  The teacher collects the scripts for a final check.

VARIATION

After students have finished rewriting their stories in the three 'Flashback' groups,
each group in turn dictates a version to the teacher who writes it on the board.
The other groups score points for making corrections.

KEY

### A Correct sequence of events

1 C  2 A  3 D  4 B
**A  Retelling the story**
The solution is to use the past perfect. One possible version would be:
    In 1975 seventy-five criminals came out of a tunnel into the local courtroom. They
    had planned to escape from Saltillo prison and had spent six months digging the
    tunnel. Finally, they were sent back to the prison.

### B Sequencing 'The least alert burglar'

1 D  2 A  3 E  4 B  5 G  6 C  7 F  8 H

# 2.13  The perfect detective

VERB FORM   Past perfect simple
AIM   Highlighting sequence using past perfect simple, past simple and connectors – *and, but, when, so, before, after, because, although, as soon as, once* (distinguishing between connectors that show sequence clearly and those that don't).
LEVEL   Upper-intermediate to advanced
TIME   35–50 minutes
MATERIALS   One copy of 'The perfect detective' for each student (page 131)

IN CLASS

## A  Finding contradictions in testimonies

1  Give each student a copy of 'The perfect detective' and ask them to read the background to the murder case.

2  As examples, read two of the testimonies with the class, e.g. that of Sir John Hall, which contains no contradiction, and that of Prince John, which has a contradiction.

3  Students read the remaining testimonies and find the other four contradictory testimonies.

4  Students compare solutions.

5  Go over the contradictions with the class.

## B  Grammar summaries (page 132)

1  Ask students to complete the grammar summaries A and B using the testimonies of all the characters as data to work from. They discuss the answers together.

2  Go over the answers with the class.

KEY

### A  Finding contradictions in testimonies

Contradictory Testimonials
Lord Aston: *when I'd left* and *when I left*
The Duchess of Crewe: *The terrible act had happened when . . .* and *the murder happened at eleven, when . . .*
Prince John: *I left* and *I'd left*
Sheila Baker: *I left* and *I'd left*
Colonel Kernel: *I left* and *I'd left*

### B  Grammar summaries

A  1 after  2 because  3 before  4 although  5 as soon as  6 so  7 once
a) true  b) false  c) true
B  1 when  2 but  3 and
a) true  b) true

# 2.14 Antarctica outside, Atlantis inside

VERB FORM    Past perfect continuous
AIM    Checking understanding of sequencing in the past perfect continuous
LEVEL    Upper-intermediate to advanced
TIME    20–30 minutes
MATERIALS    One copy of 'Antarctica outside, Atlantis inside' for each student (page 133)

IN CLASS

### A Prediction of content of text

1  Ask students to work in pairs and predict what they would expect to find on returning home in the following true situation:
A water pipe bursts in your house at lunchtime and you return home at 10.30 p.m. The temperature outside is minus fifteen degrees centigrade.

2  Write their predictions on the board.

3  Pre-teach: *icicles, sodden, mains, plumber, Atlantis.*

4  Ask students to read the text and to check which of their predictions were correct. Go over these on the board.

### B Sequencing task

Ask students to put the sixteen events listed into the correct chronological order. Note that many students will put a) and b) as first, when in fact they are last. This will promote lively discussion.

KEY

### B Sequencing task

a) 15  b) 16  c) 2  d) 5  e) 7  f) 6  g) 3  h) 4  i) 8  j) 9  k) 11 or 12  l) 10
m) 12 or 11  n) 14  o) 13  p) 1

# 2.15 Practice makes perfect

**2.14 'Antartica outside Atlantis inside'** should be completed before this exercise and then used for this activity.

VERB FORM    Past perfect continuous
AIM    Highlighting and summarising three uses of the past perfect continuous
LEVEL    Upper-intermediate to advanced
TIME    45 minutes
MATERIALS    One copy of 'Practice makes perfect' for each student (page 134)

IN CLASS

## A  Quiz

1  Give each student a copy of 'Practice makes perfect'.

2  Students work in pairs to decide if the given answers are appropriate or not.

3  Go over the answers with the class.

## B  Completing the chart

Ask students to work individually and enter the concepts in the chart. They then compare answers with a partner. Go over the answers with the class.

## C  Timelines option

1  If students are unfamiliar with timelines, give a few examples using the section on Timelines in the Introduction (p. 9).

2  Ask students to draw the timelines and then compare notes. Alternatively, put the timelines on the board in random order for the students to match and draw.

KEY

### A  Quiz

1 three 2 both finished and unfinished activities 3 yes 4 both sentences are possible – the first refers to a repeated action, the second refers to one interrupted action, therefore the meaning is different 5 The answer to all three is *No.* 6 correct – both are possible

### B  Completing the chart and  C  Timelines option

| Example sentence | Use | Timeline |
|---|---|---|
| a) I had just been thinking about the terrible winter of 1987, when I saw the advertisement. | Action completed shortly before another | PAST    NOW    FUTURE  ᴠᴠ X |
| b) He had been staying late at work for weeks. | Action repeated in a past period | PAST    NOW    FUTURE  ᴠᴠ ᴠᴠ ᴠᴠ |
| c) Water had been cascading through his house since lunchtime. | Action extending over a past period | PAST    NOW    FUTURE  ᴸᴠᴠᴠᴠ |

# 2.16 Perfect one liners

| | |
|---|---|
| VERB FORM | Past perfect continuous |
| AIM | Controlled practice of the past perfect continuous |
| LEVEL | Intermediate to advanced |
| TIME | 30–50 minutes |
| MATERIALS | None |

IN CLASS

A  **Stimulus–creative response**

1  Organise the class into small teams of two to four.

2  The teacher reads out one of the following prompts:
   a) When I came to see you yesterday, your cat was in the fridge.
   b) Can you explain why you bit my dog?
   c) That was my new Rolls Royce your son pushed over the cliff.
   d) You had blood all over your wedding clothes after the ceremony.
   e) You were the only one in the room before the theft.
   f) You had different coloured socks on the other day.
   g) Why did Henry VIII have his wife, Anne Boleyn, beheaded?

3  Each group then has thirty seconds to produce and write down a response using the past perfect continuous. For example:
   Prompt: When I came to see you yesterday, your cat was in the fridge.
   Response: Well, *it had been trying* to eat the fish so I put it inside.

4  The teacher goes to each group in turn and awards a point for a correct and suitable response. The response from each group must be different from any which have already been offered to win a point. On each new round, the teacher starts with a different team.

# 2.17 Man-eating shark

This activity follows on from the presentation of the past perfect continuous in 2.14 'Antartica outside Atlantis inside'

| | |
|---|---|
| VERB FORM | Past perfect continuous |
| AIM | Written practice of past perfect continuous with three uses |
| LEVEL | Upper-intermediate to advanced |
| TIME | 60 minutes |
| MATERIALS | One copy of 'Man-eating shark' for each student (page 135) |

IN CLASS

A  **Previewing the story**

1  Ask students to work in pairs or small groups and to work out four things they

would do to survive in a small rubber raft on the open sea. Ask them to estimate how many days they think they could survive.

2  Write up on the board their suggestions for survival and their estimated periods of survival.

## B | Reading and rewriting the story

1  Give each student a copy of 'Man-eating shark' and ask them to read the true story about the Baileys who survived at sea on a small rubber raft. Ask them to see which of their suggestions were followed by the Baileys and how far their estimated survival periods differed from the one in the story.

2  Refer students to the example sentences in the past perfect continuous in 'Antartica outside Atlantis inside'. Ask them to rewrite 'Man-eating shark' to incorporate three similar sentences in the past perfect continuous. They should not write more than ninety words and they should not change any of the facts in the original story.

3  Students exchange scripts for checking before handing them to the teacher for correction.

KEY

### B | Reading and rewriting the story

There are of course several different ways of rewriting the story – here is just one possibility:

Michael Bailey and his wife had been drifting for 118 days in a rubber raft in the Pacific before they were rescued by a Korean trawler. They had been sailing between Mexico and the Galapagos Islands in 1972 and had just been having lunch when their boat was hit by a whale. Their yacht had been filling with water for an hour before they took to their raft. To survive they had been catching and eating small sharks, seagulls, and turtles, and drinking rainwater.

# 2.18  Union jacks

| | |
|---|---|
| VERB FORM | Past simple, past continuous, past perfect simple, past perfect continuous |
| AIM | Correction of errors of use in the four past tenses |
| LEVEL | Upper-intermediate to advanced |
| TIME | 45 minutes |
| MATERIALS | One copy of 'Union jacks' for each student (page 136) |

IN CLASS

## A | Teams correct errors

1  Arrange students in groups of two to four.

2  Give each student a copy of 'Union jacks' and ask the teams to decide which sentences contain errors.

3  Within their teams, the students agree on the corrections necessary.

## B Team competition

1 Each team takes a turn to select a flag and offer their corrected version.

2 They receive a point for correction or identifying a sentence as correct.

3 If they make a mistake, the turn passes to the next team.

KEY

### B Correcting errors

1 *Have you ordered* my bacon ...
2 Correct  3 Correct  4 Correct  5 I *burnt/burned* my hands when I ...
6 He *was driving* his Ford at sixty mph, when ... The man was the faster driver and also did the impossible.  7 I *had* been trying to brush up ...  8 Correct
9 Leslie and Lesley had finally *rung* me at eight to ...  10 Correct
11 John ordered first and more than Andrew.  12 I *saw* you yesterday morning ...
13 – it *fell* in because it had/had had a heart attack.  14 The rest of Europe *had had* a decimal system for centuries ....  15 I *tried/had tried* it on a previous visit.

# 2.19  Story swop

| | |
|---|---|
| VERB FORM | All past tenses |
| AIM | Communicative practice, exchanging narratives |
| LEVEL | Intermediate to advanced |
| TIME | 80 minutes |
| MATERIALS | One copy of 'Story swop' for every four students (page 137). Cut up the story sheet into sets of four stories. |

IN CLASS

## A Assigning texts and reading stories

1 Arrange the class into groups of four and assign each student a letter – A, B, C, or D. If there are spare students, then they work in a pair and are assigned the same letter.

2 Tell the students they are going to read some true stories and that they will then tell the stories to each other. Hand out the stories: all the A students receive-story A, 'Girl had bullets in her scalp', all the B students receive story B, 'Getting the wind up', and so on.

3 Tell the students to read the story they have been given. The teacher can circulate and give help where necessary.

## B Swopping stories

Ask the students to put their texts away and then get them to swop stories in six rounds as follows:

**Round One**    A tells B about 'Girl had bullet in her scalp'
                 C tells D about 'Head case'

| Round Two | B tells C about 'Girl had bullet in her scalp' |
| | D tells A about 'Head case' |
| **Round Three** | C tells D about 'Girl had bullet in her scalp' |
| | A tells B about 'Head case' |
| **Round Four** | B tells A about 'Getting the wind up' |
| | D tells C about 'The worst bank robbers' |
| **Round Five** | A tells D about 'Getting the wind up' |
| | C tells B about 'The worst bank robbers' |
| **Round Six** | D tells C about 'Getting the wind up' |
| | B tells A about 'The worst bank robbers' |

The teacher can call out the instructions for each round or write the complete procedure for the six rounds on the board.

## C Writing up stories

1 Ask students to write up the following stories:
   A writes up 'The worst bank robbers'
   B writes up 'Head case'
   C writes up 'Getting the wind up'
   D writes up 'Girl had bullet in her scalp'

   The students should use each of the following tenses at least once: past simple; past continuous; past perfect simple or continuous

2 In their original groups, students exchange scripts and discuss inaccuracies, grammatical and factual.

# Section 3
# Futures

## 3.1 How simple is the future simple?

VERB FORM Future simple
AIM Highlighting the *will*/*shall* distinction
LEVEL Upper-intermediate to advanced
TIME 20 minutes
MATERIALS One copy of 'How simple is the future simple?' for each student (page 138)

IN CLASS

### *Will* against *shall* in the future simple

1 Ask the class to work individually to read the questions and to answer them with reference to the extracts on *will* and *shall*.

2 Students compare answers with a partner. Go over the answers with the class.

KEY

### *Will* against *shall* in the future simple

1 True 2 True 3 False 4 True 5 False 6 True 7 True 8 This is a matter of opinion. *The Sun* seems to be following the tendency to use *will* in informal speech and writing; however, it is likely that the original words included *shall* as reported in *The Star*.

## 3.2 Funny future

VERB FORM Future simple, *going to* future, present simple, present continuous
AIM Presentation of the above forms to express the future
LEVEL Mid-intermediate to advanced
TIME 50 minutes
MATERIALS One copy of 'Funny future' for each student (pages 139–141)

IN CLASS

### A Overviewing the texts

1 Give each student a copy of 'Funny future'.

2 Ask them to read quickly through all the texts on the sheets. Can they identify which ones are jokes? Ask them to compare with a partner and explain the jokes to each other.

## B Focussing on uses

Ask students to read all the texts and answer the questions. They can work individually and then compare notes. Go over the answers.
(Section D is entitled 'Look it up' because the present simple can only be used for the future if you can look up the information on a timetable, calendar or schedule.)

## C Summarising verb forms and uses

'Decisions already made' includes plans and arrangements. These are regarded as interchangeable, in line with Swan *Practical English Usage*. 'Future as fact' embraces schedule/calendar/timetable uses and sees the present simple and future simple as interchangeable.

1 Give the students a copy of 'Summary tables' each (page 142).

2 Ask the class to complete Table 1 individually.

3 Pair off students, and get them to compare and agree on their information.

4 In pairs, complete Table 2.

5 Get students to answer the *True/False* questions at the bottom of the tables.

KEY

### A Overviewing the texts

A 1, A 2, B 1, B 2, B 3, C 1, C 2

### B Focussing on uses

A box: future simple, *going to*
  a) True b) True c) False d) True
  In these examples *will* is used to *give an opinion*.
B box: present continuous, *going to*, future simple
  a) The decisions in 1 and 2 *have already been made*.
  b) The decision in 3 *is being made now*.
  In this example *will* is used to *make a spontaneous decision*.
C In these examples *will* is used to state a fact.
D X = Calendar events: 1, 2
  Y = Schedules: 3, 4, 7
  Z = Timetables: 5, 6

### C Summarising verb forms and uses

| Table 1: Verb form | Use |
| --- | --- |
| 1 future simple | prediction |
| 2 *going to* | prediction |
| 3 *going to* | prediction: certain to happen |
| 4 present continuous | decisions already made |
| 5 *going to* | decisions already made |
| 6 future simple | spontaneous decision |
| 7 future simple | future as fact |
| 8 present simple | future as fact |

**Table 2: Uses**
1 prediction (but not if certain to happen), spontaneous decision, future as fact
2 all predictions, decisions already made
3 decisions already made
4 future as fact
a) False b) True

# 3.3  Journalist of the future

**3.3 'Funny futures'** should be completed before this exercise.

VERB FORM   Future simple, *going to* future, present simple, present continuous
AIM   Controlled practice of the four future forms
LEVEL   Mid-intermediate to advanced
TIME   40–50 minutes
MATERIALS   One copy of 'Journalist of the future' for each student (page 143)

IN CLASS

## A  Warm-up

1  Elicit the names of international newspapers from the class – ask for at least one from the Americas, Europe, Africa and Asia.

2  Optionally pre-teach: *Chunnel* (= Channel + Tunnel), the Channel Tunnel between England and France.

3  Give each student a copy of 'Journalist of the future' and ask them to name the country of origin of each of the six newspapers.

## B  Deciding on uses/verb forms for the future

1  Ask the students to work in pairs to assign one of the four uses of the future to each of the headlines together with a corresponding verb form. Tell the class there is no right answer, and more than one possibility for each headline but some combinations will be easier to use than others.

2  Students write the uses/verb forms in the boxes at the top of each newspaper.

## C  Writing opening sentences

1  Ask the students, either working individually or in pairs, to write an opening sentence corresponding to their chosen headline of not more than fifteen words for each of the six items. Emphasise that each sentence should be about the future. They could refer to the summary tables in 3.2 'Funny future' (p. 142) if they have worked through this activity. Otherwise, discuss with the class the possible combinations of use and verb form.

2  When the students have written their sentences, get them to exchange scripts for checking and reading before collecting them for final correction. Alternatively, get a selection of sentences written on the board by the students for correction by the class.

KEY

### A  Warm-up

Le Monde – France, Pravda – Soviet Union, Folha de São Paulo – Brazil, The Indian Times – India, Al Ahram – Egypt, The Times – Great Britain

### C  Writing opening sentences: suggested answers

There are of course endless possibilities for opening sentences. Here are some examples:

Le Monde: (future as fact/present simple) *The second stage of building the Chunnel starts tomorrow.*
Pravda: (future as fact/future simple) *The two superpowers will have more talks on arms control next week.*
Folha de São Paulo: (decision already made/present continuous) *The Brazilian President is leaving politics after five years in office.*
The Indian Times: (spontaneous decision/future simple) *I'll take it! said Soria, India's top actress when offered a new part in Ray's forthcoming film.*
Al Ahram: (decision already made/going to) *Beirut airport is going to be reopened in a few days time.*
The Times: (prediction/future simple) *Today it will be extremely cold and there will be snow showers in the north.*

# 3.4 Double date

VERB FORM    Future simple, *going to* future, present simple, present continuous
AIM    Information exchange practising the four future forms
LEVEL    Intermediate to upper-intermediate
TIME    40 minutes
MATERIALS    One copy of 'Double date' for every four students (page 144–5). Cut up the diaries in sets of four.

IN CLASS

### A Pre-teaching

If necessary, pre-teach: *dye, nursery* (for plants), *stepmother, pick up* (= collect)

### B Setting up groups

1 Arrange the class in groups of four students.

2 Give each student in each group one of the sets of four diaries. This means that in each group, one student receives a diary sheet with entries for Bill, one with entries for Henrietta, one with entries for Tom, and one with entries for Edward.

3 Each student takes on the role of the character for whom they have entries.

### C Information exchange

1 Within each group of four, students work in pairs, changing partners twice until all the information has been exchanged, e.g. Bill to Tom: *Are you doing anything at 8.00 on Wednesday?*
Tom: *No, I'm free.*

2 The aim for each student is to find out who has a double engagement by entering the plans of each other character against the blank times 'next Wednesday'.

3 The teacher notes errors to be corrected at the end.

**Errors**

In practice it has been found that the following problematic errors frequently crop up during the exercise:

a) *I'll do nothing at eight.*
*I do nothing at eight.*

By definition you cannot put nothing on a schedule; you can of course plan to do nothing – *I'm not going to do anything/I'm not doing anything at eight.*

b) *I have dinner with Mum and Dad at seven.*

This is grammatically correct as it is part of a schedule but the register is too formal in the context of 'Mum and Dad'. The correct answer would be *I'm having/going to have dinner...*

c) *I'll expect a phone call at ten. I expect a phone call at ten. I'm going to expect a phone call at ten.*

The phone call is at ten but the expecting has already begun. The correct utterance would be *I'm expecting a phone call at ten.* – present continuous with present meaning.

d) *I take the dog for a walk tonight.*

Grammatically correct but not something you would see as part of a schedule.

KEY

> ### C  Information exchange
> Henrietta has arranged to meet Bill at the restaurant at six and to go to the cinema with Tom and Mary at the same time.

# 3.5  Anyone for cricket?

| | |
|---|---|
| VERB FORM | Future simple, *going to* future, present simple, present continuous |
| AIM | Correcting errors of use in the four verb forms |
| LEVEL | Mid-intermediate to advanced |
| TIME | 50 minutes |
| MATERIALS | One copy of 'Anyone for cricket?' for each student (page 146). |

IN CLASS

### A  Previewing the text

Ask the students what they know about cricket, if anything.

### B  Team competition

1  Arrange the class in groups of three to four, giving them names such as 'bowlers', 'fielders', 'batsmen' and 'umpires'.

2  Give each student a copy of 'Anyone for cricket?'

3  Ask students to work individually to read the conversation and identify any incorrect uses of verb form.

4  Students compare notes within their groups and agree on corrections.

5  In turn teams identify errors and receive a point. They receive a further point for a successful correction and another point if they can explain the reason for the correction.

6  Groups continue until all eight mistakes have been identified, corrected and explained.

KEY

| B | **Competition** |
|---|---|

3    Then *I'll* understand it better.
6    I think *he'll make* a mistake in a minute and the ball *will hit* his wicket.
16   *It's going to rain* tomorrow.
18   Don't worry, *I'll* explain it to you when . . .
20   *He'll* probably *do* it again soon.
21   You mean you are *going to explain* the game to me again?! It's *going to rain* very soon.

# 3.6  Who will be dancing in the streets?

VERB FORM  Future continuous
AIM  Highlighting the form of the future continuous, correction of errors of form
LEVEL  Mid-intermediate to upper-intermediate
TIME  20–30 minutes
MATERIALS  One copy of 'Who will be dancing in the streets?' for each student (page 147)

IN CLASS

## A | Identifying topic

1  Give each student a copy of 'Who will be dancing in the streets?' with the substitution table folded under.

2  Ask them to try to identify as much as they can about what is being discussed from the speech bubbles.

## B | Identifying and correcting errors

1  Students work in pairs to identify which speech bubbles contain errors of form (not use) and how to correct them.

2  Go over the answers.

## C | Completing substitution table

Ask students to complete the substitution table. Go over it with the class.

KEY

### A  Identifying topic

Notting Hill Carnival in London, organised by the large Caribbean community. It is now Europe's largest street festival.

### B  Correcting errors

1 Correct 2 Do you know the *police will be dancing . . . if/that/whether* the police *will be dancing . . .* 3 Correct 4 Once again they will be *celebrating* this annual event . . . 5 The poor will *be* imitating the rich . . . 6 The police *will be searched* for drugs and weapons by the public/the public *will be searching* the police for drugs and weapons (roles are reversed during Carnival) 7 *Won't* the steelbands be playing . . .? 8 Nobody will be working until Tuesday, *will they?* 9 Will one million people *be coming* to see it . . .? 10 Correct 11 Correct

### C  Completing substitution table

| | Europe's biggest street festival |
|---|---|
| | Next weekend in Notting Hill (just north of Hyde Park) about one million people, many of them from London's Caribbean community, |
| **Positive** **Positive contraction** | *will be* (*They'll be*) } *celebrating* Carnival, or Mas as it's called in Trinidad, the country of its origin. |
| **Negative** **Negative contraction** | The police { *will not be* taking / *won't be* taking } their duties seriously unless of course crimes are committed. |
| **Positive question** **Negative question** | *Will* they *be* dancing / *Won't* they *be* dancing } in the streets with the public? |

# 3.7  Gilbert

| | |
|---|---|
| VERB FORM | Future continuous |
| AIM | Presentation of four uses of the future continuous |
| LEVEL | Upper-intermediate to advanced |
| TIME | 25 minutes |
| MATERIALS | One copy of 'Gilbert' for each student (page 148) |

IN CLASS

### A  Previewing the text

1  Ask students to work in pairs to decide which parts of the world suffer from hurricanes and what precautions they would take if a hurricane was imminent.

2  Elicit the opinions from the class, and write up on the board the parts of the world and the precautions to be taken.

## B Reading the text

1 Set four reading tasks: a) Are there any parts of the world which have not been listed on the board?
   b) Are there any precautions which have not been listed on the board?
   c) Who or what is Gilbert?
   d) From which of the media does the report come?

2 Give each student a copy of 'Gilbert'.

3 Check the answers with the class.

## C Highlighting concepts of the future continuous

1 Ask the class to work individually to underline all the examples of the future continuous in the text and then to answer the questions. Make sure that students are aware that the questions refer to the sentences in the text immediately adjacent.

2 Students compare answers in pairs.

3 Go over the answers with the class.

KEY

### B Reading the text

c) a hurricane
d) radio or television

### C Highlighting concepts of the future continuous

1 period 2 yes 3 before 4 extremely frequent

# 3.8 Caribbean future

**3.7 'Gilbert'** should be completed before this exercise.

| | |
|---|---|
| VERB FORM | Future simple, future continuous |
| AIM | Summarising uses of the future continuous, contrasting future simple and future continuous |
| LEVEL | Upper-intermediate to advanced |
| TIME | 30 minutes |
| MATERIALS | One copy of 'Caribbean future' for each student (page 149) |

IN CLASS

## A Completing the chart

1 Give each student a copy of 'Caribbean future' and ask them to work individually to enter the uses in the table.

2 Ask students to compare in pairs and then go over the answers with them.

## B Timelines option

1 If students are unfamiliar with timelines, give a few examples using the section on Timelines in the Introduction (p. 9).

2 Students draw timelines and compare notes. Alternatively, put the timelines on the board in random order for students to match and draw. Go over the answers.

C **Contrasting the future simple and future continuous**

Students do the exercise in pairs. Then go over the answers with the class.

KEY

A **Completing the chart and** B **Timelines option**

| Example sentence | Use | Timeline |
|---|---|---|
| 1 We'll be reporting on Gilbert's progress . . . between ten and ten-thirty later tonight. | action through a period | PAST NOW FUTURE (10·00 10·30) |
| 2 Gilbert will be reaching the Jamaican coast at three a.m. | action at/around a point of time | PAST NOW FUTURE (3·00) |
| 3 Most people will be sleeping when it hits the island. | interrupted action | PAST NOW FUTURE (X) |
| 4 Jamaica will always be having cyclones and hurricanes. | emphasising very frequent action | PAST NOW FUTURE |

*True*

C **Contrasting the future simple and future continuous**

1 i) True – the only difference is one of subjective emphasis ii) a
2 a)
3 b) because this means that people will go to sleep when the hurricane hits the island
4 a)

# 3.9 Siesta

| | |
|---|---|
| VERB FORM | Future continuous |
| AIM | Controlled practice of future continuous |
| LEVEL | Mid-intermediate to upper-intermediate |
| TIME | 30 minutes |
| MATERIALS | One copy of 'Siesta' for each student (page 150) |

IN CLASS

A **Pre-teaching**

Pre-teach as necessary: *siesta, brunch* (= breakfast + lunch), *transcendental meditation, shuttle launch, shelter* (n), *carnation, drop in* (= visit), *tennis seed, withdraw* (from a competition), *tournament.*

## B Team competition

1 Arrange the students in groups of three to four.

2 Give each student a copy of 'Siesta'.

3 The first group chooses one of the ten situations and reads it out to the second group. Example: *How will I recognise you at the station?*

4 The second group finds a prompt which fits logically with the situation and then produces a sentence in the future continuous. Example: *I'll be wearing a pink carnation in my jacket.* If it is correct, they win a point. If not, they forfeit their turn to the next group who can win a bonus point before having their own turn.

5 The second group now reads out one of the remaining sentences for the third group and so on. The game continues until all of the situations have generated correct responses.

VARIATION

When sentences are completed, ask students to say whether there's a difference between the future continuous and the future simple.
For example:
In 7, there's a difference in meaning depending on tense.
a) *I wouldn't ring our Spanish branch immediately after lunch; they'll be having a siesta.*
   (You'll interrupt them.)
b) *I wouldn't ring our Spanish branch immediately after lunch; they'll have a siesta.*
   (They'll have a siesta as a result of your call.)
However in 4, both tenses produce virtually the same meaning.
a) *He won't be playing in the tournament this year.*
b) *He won't play in the tournament this year.*

KEY

### B Competition: possible answers

1 I will be wearing a carnation in my jacket.
2 I will be practising transcendental meditation then.
3 We will be flying at 15,000 metres.
4 You won't be having any more money problems.
5 So he won't be playing in the tournament this year.
6 I will be having brunch then.
7 They'll be having a siesta.
8 One million spectators will be watching when the shuttle is launched.
9 He'll always be having accidents.
10 I'll be sitting in my underground shelter.

# 3.10  The perfect future for the kangaroo?

| | |
|---|---|
| VERB FORM | Future perfect simple, future perfect continuous |
| AIM | Highlighting of form of future perfect simple and future perfect continuous, correction of errors of form |
| LEVEL | Upper-intermediate to advanced |
| TIME | 30 minutes |
| MATERIALS | One copy of 'The perfect future for the kangaroo?' for each student (page 151) |

IN CLASS

## A  Previewing the text

1  Ask the students to estimate the following:
   a) What is the population of Australia?
   b) What is the kangaroo population?
   c) Are the kangaroos in any danger?
   d) How many kinds are there?
   Put the students' estimates on the board.
2  Give each student a copy of 'The perfect future for the kangaroo?'

3  Ask students to read quickly through the text to check the estimates on the board.

## B  Groups locate errors of form

1  Arrange students in groups of two to four.

2  Elicit an example of the future perfect simple and continuous from the class.

3  Ask the students to find eight errors of form (not use) in the text in the future perfect simple and continuous. Students work in groups to identify and correct them.

## C  Correcting errors

In turn, groups receive a point for locating an error and an extra point for correcting it. If they are unsuccessful at correction, the next team has a chance to win a bonus point before taking their own turn.

## D  Completing substitution table

Ask students to complete the substitution table of the forms of the future perfect simple and continuous (page 152).

KEY

### C  Correcting errors

L. 14: will have *shot* dead 2 L. 18: will also have *been* shooting 3. L. 19: that will *have been* shot will be much higher 4 L. 23: will *have died* out. 5 L. 23: how many *will have* been hit 6 L. 27: How many thousands of years will *the kangaroo have been living there*? 7 L. 28: Why so many people will have *ignored* this 8 L. 31 year, *won't they*?

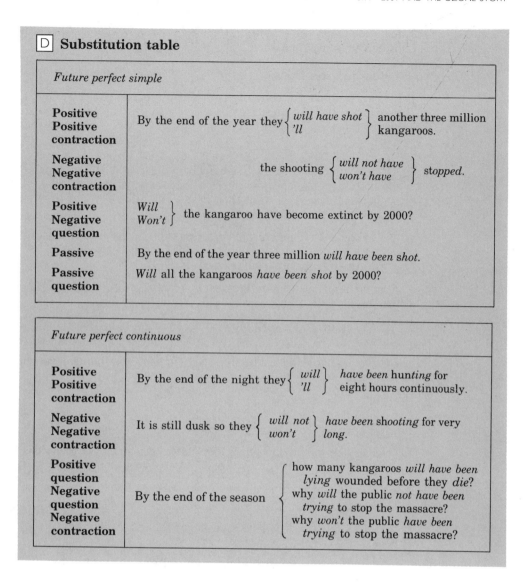

D  **Substitution table**

*Future perfect simple*

| Positive<br>Positive<br>contraction | By the end of the year they { *will have shot* / *'ll* } another three million kangaroos. |
| Negative<br>Negative<br>contraction | the shooting { *will not have* / *won't have* } stopped. |
| Positive<br>Negative<br>question | *Will* / *Won't* } the kangaroo have become extinct by 2000? |
| Passive | By the end of the year three million *will have been* shot. |
| Passive<br>question | *Will* all the kangaroos *have been* shot by 2000? |

*Future perfect continuous*

| Positive<br>Positive<br>contraction | By the end of the night they { *will* / *'ll* } have been hun*ting* for eight hours continuously. |
| Negative<br>Negative<br>contraction | It is still dusk so they { *will not* / *won't* } have been shoot*ing* for very long. |
| Positive<br>question<br>Negative<br>question<br>Negative<br>contraction | By the end of the season { how many kangaroos *will have been* lying wounded before they *die*? why *will* the public *not have been* trying to stop the massacre? why *won't* the public *have been* trying to stop the massacre? |

# 3.11  2001 and the ozone story

| VERB FORM | Future perfect simple |
| AIM | Presentation of four uses of the future perfect simple |
| LEVEL | Upper-intermediate to advanced |
| TIME | 30 minutes |
| MATERIAL | One copy of '2001 and the ozone story' for each student (page 153) |

IN CLASS

A  **Previewing the texts**

1  Tell the class that the sun gives off ultra-violet rays which are harmful to humans.

2 Ask them what they think protects us from ultra-violet rays and why this protection is disappearing.

B Reading the texts

1 Give each student a copy of '2001 and the ozone story' and ask them to find the answers to the two questions in A above by reading the mini-texts on the top half of the worksheet.

2 Go over the answers.

3 Ask the students to work individually and read the three paragraphs (1–3) on the bottom half of the worksheet to decide which of the three is, in their opinion and based on what they have read, most likely to have happened by 2000.

4 Ask students to compare opinions and then invite class discussion.

C Focussing on time reference

1 Ask the students to underline examples of the future perfect simple in paragraphs 1 to 3.

2 Ask the students to work individually to answer the questions 1 to 3 below the texts.

3 Get the class to compare their answers in pairs and then go over the answers.

KEY

B Reading the texts

The ozone layer protects us from ultra-violet rays. This layer of ozone is being damaged by CFCs used in industry. CFCs are found in aerosols, foam packaging, air conditioning and refrigeration systems.

C Focussing on time reference

1 a) past   b) yes   c) a short time before the end of the century
2 we don't know - at an indefinite time
3 several actions

# 3.12   Ozone – a thing of the past or the future?

**2001 and the ozone story** should be completed before doing this exercise.

| | |
|---|---|
| VERB FORM | Future perfect simple, future simple |
| AIM | Highlighting and summarising four uses of the future perfect simple, contrasting future perfect simple and future simple |
| LEVEL | Upper-intermediate to advanced |
| TIME | 25 minutes |
| MATERIALS | One copy of 'Ozone – a thing of the past or future?' for each student (page 154) |

IN CLASS

## A Completing the chart

1 Give each student a copy of 'Ozone – a thing of the past or future?.'

2 Ask the class to work individually to enter the uses in the chart. Then they can compare notes with a neighbour. Go over the answers.

## B Timelines option

1 Ask students to draw the timelines against each example. If students are unfamiliar with timelines, give a few examples using the section on Timelines in the Introduction (p. 9).

2 When they have drawn the timelines, ask them to compare in pairs. Alternatively, draw the timelines in random order on the board for students to match and draw. Go over the answers.

## C Contrasting future perfect simple and future simple

Students work in pairs to contrast the sets of sentences. Go over the answers.

KEY

## A Completing the chart and B Timelines option

| Example sentence | Use | Timeline |
|---|---|---|
| 1 In September 1999 the agreement will have been in force for twelve years. | situation extending over a future period | PAST   NOW   FUTURE  1987 ⌇⌇⌇ 1999 |
| 2 By the year 2000 we will have just avoided a catastrophe. | action completed shortly before a future point | PAST   NOW   FUTURE  2000  x↓ |
| 3 By the end of the century we will have found a simple solution to the problem of the ozone layer. | action completed at an indefinite time in a future period | PAST   NOW   FUTURE  ? 2000  x |
| 4 Environmentalists fear that more and more holes will have appeared by the year 2000. | action repeated at indefinite times in a future period | PAST   NOW   FUTURE  ? 2000  xxx |

## C Contrasting future perfect simple and future simple

1 In a) the agreement will be already twelve years old in 1999; in b) the agreement comes into operation with effect from 1999.

2 In a) the catastrophe will be over shortly before 2000; in b) the catastrophe will be avoided in the year 2000 itself; (*just* in a) means a short time before 2000, in b) it means *narrowly*.

3 a)

4 a)

# 3.13 By the time you're 100…

| | |
|---|---|
| VERB FORM | Future perfect simple |
| AIM | Controlled practice of the future perfect simple |
| LEVEL | Intermediate to upper-intermediate |
| TIME | 20–30 minutes |
| MATERIALS | One copy of 'By the time you're 100 …' for each student (page 155) |

IN CLASS

## A Estimating the answers

1 Divide the class into groups A and B.

2 Give each student a copy of 'By the time you're 100…'

3 Within the groups the students decide which of the estimates they think are correct.

## B Pairs comparison

1 Pair students off, one student in each pair from group A and one from group B.

2. The students in each pair find out the estimates agreed on in the other group. They have to use *wh-* questions, e. g. *How many…?, How much…?, How far…?*, etc., and they have to use the future perfect simple, e. g. *How many potatoes will the average English person have eaten by the time they're 100?* The teacher monitors for errors and then goes over the errors and the answers.

## C Personalisation

1 Ask the students to work out individually estimates for their own consumption of potatoes, hours slept, cups of tea drunk, etc.

2 Get students to report their estimates in small groups.

KEY

## B Pairs comparison

1 9,300 kilos of potatoes 2 29 years 3 169,725 cups 4 56,568 hours 5 31,025 newspapers 6 2,222 days 7 708,100 times 8 £40,000 on tins at 1988 prices 9 all three are the same

# 3.14 Problems, problems, problems!

| | |
|---|---|
| VERB FORM | Future perfect continuous |
| AIM | Presentation of three uses of the future perfect continuous |
| LEVEL | Upper-intermediate to advanced |
| TIME | 30 minutes |
| MATERIALS | One copy of 'Problems, problems, problems!' for each student (page 156) |

IN CLASS

## A | Optional Pre-teaching

Pre-teach: *seep*

## B | Problem-solving and sentence reconstruction

1 Arrange the class in small groups of two to four and give each student a copy of 'Problems, problems, problems!'

2 Ask the class to work individually to read the three situations to try to work out what they are and to unscramble the jumbled sentences. (Tell them not to look at the questions on the right yet.) They can then discuss solutions within their groups.

3 Invite a cross-group comparison of ideas and unscrambled sentences and discuss the answers with the class.

## C | Highlighting time reference

Tell the class they are going to answer questions on the use of the future perfect continuous. Get them to work individually to answer the questions on the sentences they have just unscrambled. Then discuss the answers with the class.

KEY

### B | Problem-solving and sentence reconstruction

1 Situation: A and B are trapped in a car submerged underwater and have to wait until the water level in the car has risen to maximum so that the pressure in the car will then equal the pressure on the door which can then be opened.
Sentence: *The water will have been seeping in for long enough by then.*

2 Situation: B is giving A advice on the phone about someone who has just had an epileptic fit.
Sentence: *When you get in, he will probably have just been swallowing his tongue.*

3 Situation: B is taking his twelfth driving test next Thursday. A warns him to get the three-point turn manouvre right – a standard part of the test procedure.
Sentence: *I'll have been taking tests for six years by next Thursday!*

### C | Highlighting time reference

1 a) yes b) yes c) yes d) after 'a few more minutes'
2 a) the man will swallow his tongue first b) a short time c) just
3 a) a few days short of six years ago b) yes, he is taking his next test on Thursday
c) several repeated actions d) a period of time extending from six years ago up to next Thursday

# 3.15  Perfection at last

**3.15 'Problems, problems, problems!'** should be completed before this exercise.

| | |
|---|---|
| VERB FORM | Future perfect continuous and future perfect simple |
| AIM | Summarising uses of future perfect continuous, contrasting future perfect continuous and future perfect simple |
| LEVEL | Upper-intermediate to advanced |
| TIME | 20 minutes |
| MATERIALS | One copy of 'Perfection at last' for each student (page 157) |

IN CLASS

## A  Completing the chart

1 Ask the students to work individually to enter the concepts in the chart and to answer the *True/False* question. They then compare answers.

2 Discuss the answers with the class.

## B  Timelines option

1 If students are unfamiliar with timelines, give a few examples, using the section on Timelines in the Introduction (p. 9).

2 Students draw timelines for each example sentence. Alternatively, put timelines on the board in random order for students to match and draw.

## C  Contrasting future perfect simple and future perfect continuous

Students answer the questions and compare answers. Discuss the answers with the class.

KEY

## A  Completing the chart and  B  Timelines option

| Example sentence | Use | Timeline |
|---|---|---|
| Wait a few more minutes. The water will have been seeping in for long enough by then. | action continuing up to a future point | PAST    NOW    FUTURE |
| When you get in, he will have just been swallowing his tongue. | action completed shortly before a future point | PAST    NOW    FUTURE |
| I'll have been taking tests for six years by next Thursday. | actions repeated in a period before a future point | PAST    NOW    FUTURE  x x x x x x x |

*True*

## C  Contrasting future perfect simple and future continuous

i) True ii) a, c, e

# 3.16 What future?

| | |
|---|---|
| VERB FORM | Future simple, future continuous, future perfect simple, future perfect continuous |
| AIM | Correction of errors of use in the four future verb forms |
| LEVEL | Upper-intermediate to advanced |
| TIME | 40 minutes |
| MATERIALS | One copy of 'What future?' for each student (page 158) |

IN CLASS

### A  Teams correct errors

1  Arrange the class in small groups of two to four.

2  Give each student a copy of 'What future?'

3  Teams work together to decide which of the sentences 1–10 contain errors of use of future forms. They then agree on correct versions.

### B  Team competition

1  Teams take turns to select a sentence.

2  They receive one point for identifying a correct or incorrect sentence and one more point if they can successfully correct a sentence with a mistake in it. If they are unsuccessful, the turn passes to the next team who take over the previous team's sentence for a bonus point before continuing with its own turn.

KEY

### B  Team competition

1  the forests *will have already gone*
2  Correct.
3  They will *have cut down and burned/burnt* all the trees
4  Correct
5  Many people will *be expecting/have expected* the disaster
6  *They will have destroyed* thousands
7  will have been increasing dramatically *for* 20 years
8  when they *finish/have finished* burning
9  Correct
10  I will have *read* it

# 3.17 Futuristic city?

| | |
|---|---|
| VERB FORM | Future perfect simple, future perfect continuous, future simple, future continuous |
| AIM | Communicative practice of four verb forms with future reference, contrast of these verb forms |
| LEVEL | Upper-intermediate to advanced |
| TIME | 30 minutes |
| MATERIALS | One copy of 'Futuristic city?' (pages 159–160 for each pair of students; Divide the sheets into the two texts, A and B. |

IN CLASS

## A  Previewing the text

Ask the class which cities are the largest in the world; ask them what particular problems they face and what problems they will encounter in the future.

## B  Grouping the class and setting a reading task

1  Arrange the class in two groups, A and B.

2  Give each student in group A a copy of 'Futuristic city?: Text A,' and each student in group B a copy 'Futuristic city?: Text B'

3  Ask the students to work individually to complete the six questions.

4  Students compare with others in the same group.

5  The teacher goes over the answers with each group.

## C  Information exchange and story comparison

1  Ask the students to fold their sheets so that only the information boxes are visible.

2  Pair students off, one from group A with one from group B.

3  Ask the pairs to compare versions of the story using the information boxes as a prompt and to find four differences between their versions.

4  Go over the differences with the class.

KEY

## B  Reading task

Text A: 1a) almost 30 million 2a) 1994 3b) 1980 4c) no information 5a) 12,000 tons each day 6b) before the turn of the century
Text B: 1b) 30 million 2b) sometime in 1995 3c) before 2000 but we don't know exactly when 4a) before the year 2000 5a) 12,000 tons each day 6a) only at the turn of the century

## C  Information exchange and story comparison

Text A:
1  In 2000 the population *will be reaching* 30 million.
2  The city *will have run out* of water by 1995
3  By 2000 the city *will have been* slowly *sinking* for the last twenty years
4  At the turn of the century many people *will already be dying*

Text B:
1  *will have reached 30 million*
2  *will run out in* 1995
3  *will have sunk* another thirty cms or more
4  *will start to die*

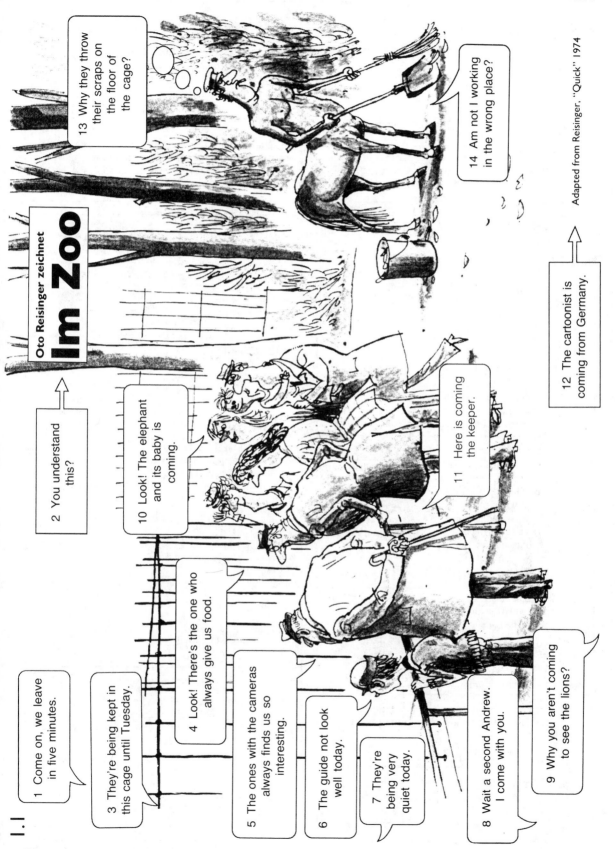

Adapted from Reisinger, "Quick" 1974

Oto Reisinger zeichnet

**Im Zoo**

1.1

# 1.2 – Mini-contexts

Look at the following examples of the present simple tense and answer the questions.

**1** a) Complete the dialogue.
**John:** _____ usually _____ at Christmas?
**Dave:** I normally go to my parents' house.

b) Is Dave talking about
   i) one specific Christmas?
   ii) Christmas holidays in general?

**2** a) Which machine are they talking about below? Tick one.

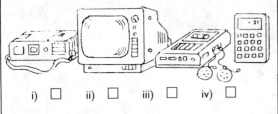

i) ☐   ii) ☐   iii) ☐   iv) ☐

b) Complete the dialogue.
**Alan:** _____ ?
**Jill:** Well, you press the eject button and then you put the tape in. Then you press the start and record buttons at the same time.

**3** What is the missing word?
**A:** Excuse me, I wonder if you can help me. I want to go to Brighton on Saturday and I want to arrive about midday.
**B:** About midday? There's a slow train that _____ at 10.00. It gets in at 11.45.

| London → Brighton | |
|---|---|
| London Victoria | ⊖ 178 d |
| Clapham Junction | d |
| Bedford | 52 d |
| Luton | 52 ◀ d |
| St. Albans | 52 d |
| Kings Cross Thameslink | ⊖ 52 d |
| St.Pauls Thameslink | 52 d |
| London Blackfriars | ⊖ 52 d |
| London Bridge | ⊖ d |
| East Croydon | 178 a |
| Purley | d |
| Coulsdon South | d |
| Merstham | d |

**4** Put the words in the correct order.

travels    about    107,000
hour    km    The    at
Earth    an

**5** Does this suggest a temporary or a permanent address?

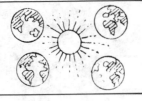

**THE AUTHOR:**
**Joasceline** lives in London with her husband, journalist and broadcaster David Dimbleby, and their three children.

**6** a) Who is speaking?
   b) Who is he/she speaking to?
   c) Why is he/she speaking?

. . . Manchester City once more. Baker plays it up the line for Tolmey. Tolmey fires a shot but it's deflected. Keagan tries to pass it out to Beardsley but doesn't succeed . . .

# The Guardian

Australia mourns

AUSTRALIA is holding a weekend of national mourning for the 70 victims of the bush fires. An appeal has been launched for 8,000 others left homeless. **Page 6.**

**7** a) What is The Guardian?
   _____

   b) What tenses are these?
   _____
   _____

   c) They refer to the same event; why are two tenses used?
   _____
   _____

## Two boys die on mountain

**By a Staff Reporter**

Two boys believed to be from London died and seven others were injured in the Snowdonia mountain range yesterday. The boys were roped together when one fell while on Craig-Yr-Ysfa.

North Wales police said that night the boys were too confused to give full details of the accident or from where they came. One boy walked five miles

   d) What tenses are these?
   _____
   _____

   e) They refer to the same event; why are two tenses used?
   _____
   _____

**8** a) **Dave:** Peter tells me you start your holidays on Saturday.
   **John:** That's right. We're going to Venice for a week.
   Does the verb *tells* refer to
   i) the time Dave is speaking?
   ii) the recent past?
   iii) the distant past?
   b) Is the trip already booked? _____

**9 Rosemary:** Don't forget to send me a postcard (when you get there)

**Andrew:** No, of course not, I'll send you a card of the Eiffel Tower (as soon as I arrive.)

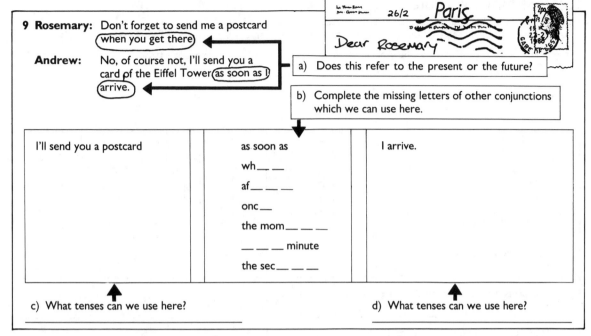

Dear Rosemary

Paris 26/2

a) Does this refer to the present or the future?

b) Complete the missing letters of other conjunctions which we can use here.

| I'll send you a postcard | as soon as | I arrive. |
|---|---|---|
| | wh __ __ | |
| | af __ __ __ | |
| | onc __ | |
| | the mom __ __ __ | |
| | __ __ __ minute | |
| | the sec __ __ __ | |

c) What tenses can we use here?
_____

d) What tenses can we use here?
_____

---

**10 Penny:** John, have you heard the one about the swimming pool?
**John:** No.
**Penny:** Well, there's this man in a swimming pool and he goes to the top of the diving board and he's just about to dive off when an attendant comes rushing along and says, 'There's no water in the pool.' 'That's alright,' says the man. 'I can't swim anyway!'

a) What does '*the one*' refer to?
b) Are there any past tenses in the story? If so, what are they? If not, why not?

---

**11** a) Which review is
  i) of a film?
  ii) of a TV documentary?
 b) Which tenses are used in each review and why?

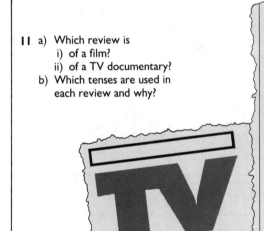

### 2.30pm All Our Yesterdays
**BERNARD BRADEN**

In 1963 Sir Winston Churchill became an honorary citizen of the United States and his son, Randolph, started a massive biography of his father that was not completed until 1988. On television, politicians were shocked by the satire of *That Was The Week That Was*. With film from the archives of Pathe Newsreel, ITN, BBC and Granada Television.

FILM RESEARCH
GRAHAM MURRAY
RESEARCH WALLEN MATTHIE
DIRECTOR MIKE BECKER
PRODUCER MIKE MURPHY

### 8.30pm NEW Legwork
**MARGARET COLIN**

First in a new thriller series introducing beautiful private eye Claire McGarron, who runs her New York business with a little help from her police lieutenant brother. In this opening episode Claire becomes involved in murder and drugs smuggling when a client is killed as he is about to pay her the money he owes her.

*Claire McGarron*
  Margaret Colin
*Terrance Considine*
  Timothy Carhart
*Haddix Bowman*
  Peter Crombie

# 1.2 – Summary Table

future time clauses    instructions    sports commentary – rapid actions    scientific facts
reporting verbs: recent past    newspaper headlines: past events    permanent situations
jokes    habits/routines    fictional plots    personal timetable/schedule
newspaper headlines: present events of short duration    public timetable/schedule

| Example sentence | General time | Present – at the time of speaking | Past | Future | No time | Use/function |
|---|---|---|---|---|---|---|
| 1   I usually go up to my parents' house. | | | | | | |
| 2   You press the eject button and then . . . | | | | | | |
| 3   There's a slow train that leaves at 10.00. | | | | | | |
| 4   The Earth travels at about 107,000 km an hour. | | | | | | |
| 5   Josceline lives in London with her husband. | | | | | | |
| 6   Baker plays it up the line for Tolmey. | | | | | | |
| 7   a)  Australia mourns | | | | | | |
|      b)  Two boys die on mountain | | | | | | |
| 8   a)  Peter tells me . . . | | | | | | |
|      b)  . . . you start your holidays on Saturday. | | | | | | |
| 9   I'll definitely send one as soon as I arrive. | | | | | | |
| 10  There's this man in a swimming pool and he goes to the top of the diving board. | | | | | | |
| 11  Claire becomes involved in murder. | | | | | | |

The present simple is mainly used to talk about present
action in progress at the time of speaking.       **True/False?**

# 1.3 – Personality

PART A

# MY KIND OF DAY

PART B

*'Island life is so idyllic, I sometimes wish my job could keep me here forever'*

ALTHOUGH I OWN a two-up-and-two-down cottage in Stratford-upon-Avon, I spend as much time here in Jersey as I can before we start filming a *Bergerac* series, to get into the feel of it, and as much time here as possible afterwards, to recover. So that tends to add up to almost the whole year. I return to Stratford from time to time as well. But my daughter, Emma, who is 19 going on 40, you know the kind, is here to boss me around.

The great joy of living in Jersey is that you are always close to the sea and there's no better way of starting the day than having a swim. So in the summer I try to climb out of bed at about half past six – I tend to cower longer under the duvet during the winter months – get dressed and take the dog down to the beach in the car. Alice is an indefinable sort of dog – mongrel is putting it a bit high, I think – but she has a great capacity to enjoy herself.

I then go straight on to the film unit for breakfast, what we call a full house: eggs, bacon and whatever else is going – so I just put on whatever clothes I am required to wear on set. But over the years I've noticed that what I wear as John Nettles is becoming very much the same as what I wear as Jim Bergerac.

In fact, looking at this lot, only the socks are my own – the sweater, trousers and shoes belong to the BBC. I daresay I'll return them one of these days!

We do have a permanent location on the island but we film all over the place, so I set off in whatever direction I have to. By and large, I can move around the island without any particular difficulty. I suppose I am well known, but no more than the butcher, the baker and the candlestick-maker – everyone knows each other here.

It's quite true that we put up false road signs to the various locations, deliberately disguised as the directions to building sites, but that's only to discourage the holidaymakers. It isn't meant to be unfriendly, it's just that it's difficult to film with thousands of people milling about. When we started doing the series, we all used to go on somewhere after we'd finished filming, but I found this to be a dreadful thief of time. Nowadays I usually come straight home. But I don't find it easy. I'm not one of nature's ascetics!

I've normally had lunch on the set so I don't need anything more to eat in the evening. Until I go to bed at around 11.00 pm I read, watch a bit of television – mostly the news and documentaries – and write. My first book, *Bergerac's Jersey*, came out here a couple of years ago and I'm now working on my next one. Since 1981, I've really got to know the island and its people and they're splendid folk.

The early-to-bed-early-to-rise routine only applies to weekdays, of course, and the weekend is a different story. That's the time when what's left of my youth tends to be spent prodigiously!

On Saturdays, I tend to enjoy the outside life. I love cycling, scuba diving and riding, although I must admit I'm not nature's greatest horseman. Then there's weightlifting – just to get rid of all my aggression.

Another thing I love doing is chasing up various bits of Jersey's past. It has a rich and varied history as it's caught midway between France and England. In fact, my second book is a selection of local tales as they have been told to me, myths and legends. Many of them are only kept going by word of mouth and it would be a shame if they were lost.

And Sunday means swimming, reading the papers and lunch. There are a number of excellent restaurants and I would normally meet up with friends in one of them or else I go to them or we'll eat here. When they come here, I usually appoint one of them to take charge of the kitchen while I do menial chores like peeling the spuds.

After a good bottle of wine – another good reason for staying in Jersey – the afternoon usually degenerates into a picture of laziness.

I often wonder what would happen if and when *Bergerac* was to come to an end. It would be difficult to live here and work somewhere else. But island life is so idyllic, I sometimes wish I had a respectable job which would allow me to stay here for ever!

# 1.4 – Galactic Shuttle

| DESTINATION Earth to … | DEPARTURE Times | FLIGHT TIME: Days | Hours | ARRIVAL Times | PRICE: Galactic Dollars (G$) | CRAFT | SERVICE |
|---|---|---|---|---|---|---|---|
| **Venus** | Daily 04.00 20.00 | 1 | 11 | 15.00 07.00 | G$200 | Venus Visitor | Super Shuttle |
| **Mercury** | Daily 07.00 19.00 | 4 | 8 | 15.00 03.00 | G$270 | Mercury Magic | Slow Shuttle |
| **Sun** | Daily not Sundays 12.00 | 6 | 10 | 22.00 | G$600 | Sunny Days | Standard Shuttle |
| **Mars** | Daily 05.00 | 3 | 15 | 20.00 | G$240 | Green Man | Slow Shuttle |
| **Jupiter** | Tuesdays/ Fridays 15.00 | 29 | | 15.00 | G$2,650 | Jupiter Jumbo | Slow Shuttle |
| **Saturn** | Mondays/ Thursdays 23.00 | 53 | 10 | 09.00 | G$6,200 | Seven Rings | Standard Shuttle |
| **Uranus** | Daily 02.00 | 102 | 1 | 03.00 | G$15,000 | Uranus Voyager | Super Shuttle |
| **Neptune** | Monthly first Sundays 03.30 | 174 | 3 | 06.30 | G$22,400 | King Neptune | Super Shuttle |
| **Pluto** | Monthly first Wednesdays 04.30 | 221 | 23 | 03.30 | G$31,000 | Pluto Discoverer | Super De Luxe Shuttle |
| **Earth orbits** | Daily 24.00 06.00 12.00 18.00 | | $3\frac{1}{4}$ | $3\frac{1}{4}$ hours later | G$64 | Earthling | De Luxe Shuttle |
| **Sun Sightseeing** | Daily 16.00 | 12 | 20 | 12.00 | G$1,450 | Sunshiner | De Luxe Shuttle |
| **Space Drifting** | Daily at sunrise | 3 | | At sunrise | G$350 | Cosmos Queen | Super De Luxe Shuttle |

PRICES:    All prices are given in Galactic Dollars $9(US) = G$1.
TIMES:     All times are given in S.E.T. (Standard Earth Time). Passengers will be advised on local planet time equivalents on board the shuttle.
SPEED:     Average speeds are calculated at 1 million km per hour.
STOPOVERS: We make stopovers at all planets en route.

# DISCOVER THE UNIVERSE WITH PLANET HOPPERS

| DESTINATION Earth to ... | DEPARTURE Times | FLIGHT TIME: Days Hours | | ARRIVAL Times | PRICE: Galactic Dollars (G$) | CRAFT | SERVICE |
|---|---|---|---|---|---|---|---|
| **Venus** | Daily 06.00 18.00 | 1 | 17 | 23.00 11.00 | G$150 | Venetian Goddess | Standard Shuttle |
| **Mercury** | Daily 12.00 24.00 | 3 | 21 | 09.00 21.00 | G$300 | Mercury II | Standard Shuttle |
| **Sun** | Daily 09.00 | 6 | 6 | 15.00 | G$620 | Sun Seeker | Standard Shuttle |
| **Mars** | Daily 14.00 | 3 | 6 | 20.00 | G$280 | Green Man | Standard Shuttle |
| **Jupiter** | Mondays/ Thursdays 07.00 | 26 | 8 | 15.00 | G$3,000 | By Jupiter | Standard Shuttle |
| **Saturn** | Sundays 01.00 | 53 | 10 | 11.00 | G$6,000 | Saturn Queen | Standard Shuttle |
| **Uranus** | Wednesdays 16.00 | 113˘ | 17 | 09.00 | G$14,000 | Uranus Star | Standard Shuttle |
| **Neptune** | Fortnightly Saturdays 23.00 | 181 | 18 | 17.00 | G$20,000 | Neptune Nipper | Standard Shuttle |
| **Pluto** | Monthly Sundays 08.00 | 240 | 8 | 16.00 | G$26,730 | Pluto | Standard |
| **Earth orbits** | Every hour on the hour | | 3 | 3 hours later | G$70 | Global Spinner | De Luxe Shuttle |
| **Sun Sightseeing** | Tuesdays 24.00 | 13 | | 24.00 | G$1,400 | Sun Sizzler | De Luxe Shuttle |
| **Space Drifting** | Daily 12.00 | 1–5 | | Variable | G$150 G$500 | Daily Drifter | De Luxe Shuttle |

PRICES:     All prices are given in Galactic Dollars $9(US) = G$1.
TIMES:      All times are given in S.E.T. (Standard Earth Time). Passengers will be advised on local planet time equivalents on board the shuttle.
SPEED:      Average speeds are calculated at 1 million km per hour.
STOPOVERS:  We make stopovers at all planets en route.

# 1.5 – Future action

  **A**

*Take your pick . . .*

Which of the sentences are correct and refer to the future?

a) When you'll see the film, you'll start to cry.

b) When you see the film, you'll start to cry.

c) When you'll see the film, you start to cry.

d) When you see the film, you start to cry.

**B**

| Conjunction | First future action | Second future action |
|---|---|---|
| When | a)  the kettle |  |
| As   soon   as | b)  smell fire |  |
| Until | c)  Majorca |  |
| After | d)  say that again |  |
| Before | e)  find the criminal |  |
| By   the   time | f)  rain |  |
| Once | g)  get my exam results |  |
| The   minute | h)  sun/set |  |
| The   very   second | i)  plane land |  |
| The   moment | j)  telephone box |  |
|  | k)  buy these new clothes |  |
|  | l)  finish the marathon |  |
|  | m) pilot on the plane |  |

# 1.6 – We are continuing presently: Part A

'David, I need some help with the piano!'

'Hang on, I'm putting out a note for the milkman at the moment!'

**I** a) Explain the joke
b) Is the action in progress?
c) Is the action finished?

---

'For the time being I'm spending so much of the day earning money that I don't have time to become rich!'

**2** a) Is the sentence logical?
b) *for the time being* means _____ ?
c) Is the situation temporary or permanent?
d) Is the speaker working at the time of speaking?

---

'Don't visit the English at one on a Sunday because they're usually eating roast beef and Yorkshire pudding.'

'Isn't that a bit old-fashioned? When was the last time *you* ate roast beef on a Sunday?'

**3** a) How many English families do *you* think eat a traditional Sunday lunch?
b) Do these families start their meal before or at one o'clock?
c) For these families is Sunday lunch at one a regular habit?
d) Are they eating at the time of the conversation?

---

'God I look old! I'm having my next birthday when I'm five years older!'

**4** a) Does the speaker want to be younger or older?
b) Is the speaker referring to the present, past, or future?
c) Has the speaker already made a firm decision about the date of his or her next birthday?

---

### Should we be proud of our British cool?

Mrs J. Meneell wrote to us recently telling us how uncomplaining the British are and how that made her proud to be British. We asked you if you agreed-should we be proud of our British cool, should we complain a bit more often? Here are some of your replies.

**I'm, sorry. I'm always saying sorry!**

We put up with indifference service because we don't like to make a fuss. We allow officials to get away with murder because we are too timid to query them, and we apologise even when the fault is not ours. A Danish friend said to me, "English people are always saying sorry. Why is that?" Why indeed!
- *Joni Brenner, Holloway, London.*

**5** a) Would Joni Brenner answer 'Yes' to the question in the main headline?
b) *English people are always saying sorry.* Does this suggest that this is a habit, a frequent habit, or a very frequent habit?

---

a) Ronnie was cleaning his teeth one morning. What a nuisance they are, he was thinking. Teeth are daft! Always needing cleaning – they're worse than shoes! Though shoes get muddy. At least teeth don't get muddy – not unless you start eating fields.

b) As Ronnie is cleaning his teeth one morning, he sees a message written in the toothpaste: 'HELP!' It reads, 'I AM A PRISONER IN A TOOTHPASTE FACTORY!' Later there is an even more urgent appeal: 'HELP! THERE'S NOT MUCH TIME!'

**6** a) Which tenses are these?
b) Do they refer to the same story?
c) Which text is from the blurb on the cover of the book? And which is from the story inside the book?

# 1.7 – We are continuing presently: Part B

A  Write the following uses of the present continuous in the correct place in the table.

| emphasising very frequent action | | temporary action in progress now |
| setting the scene: telling a plot | | regular action around a point of time |
| temporary situation | | future arrangement |

| Example sentence | Use | Timeline |
|---|---|---|
| 1 I'm putting out a note for the milkman at the moment. | | |
| 2 For the time being I'm spending so much of the day earning money that I don't have time to become rich. | | |
| 3 They're usually eating roast beef at one on a Sunday. | | |
| 4 I'm having my next birthday when I'm five years older. | | |
| 5 English people are always saying sorry. | | |
| 6 As Ronnie is cleaning his teeth one morning, he sees a message written in the toothpaste. | | |

B  Now complete timelines for each item in the chart.

C  1  Complete the first sentence with a suitable time expression.
   a) He puts out a note for the milkman . . .
   b) He's putting out a note for the milkman at the moment.

What is the difference in meaning between a) and b)?

2  a) I spend so much time earning money.
   b) For the time being I'm spending so much time earning money.

Which is felt to be temporary and which permanent?

3  a) The English usually eat roast beef at one on Sunday.
   b) The English are usually eating roast beef at one on Sunday.

When does the meal start in a) and in b)?

4  a) My next birthday is in five years time.
   b) I'm having my next birthday when I'm five years older.

Which is felt to be more a part of the calendar, a) or b)?

5  a) English people always say sorry.
   b) English people are always saying sorry.

Which is more critical, a) or b)?

6  a) As Ronnie cleans his teeth, he sees a message in the toothpaste.
   b) As Ronnie is cleaning his teeth, he sees a message in the toothpaste.

Does the writer emphasise that the action of cleaning teeth is in progress in a) or b)?

# Time Box
# BINGO

**1.8**

1  I'm putting out a note for the milkman at the moment.
2  I'm having my birthday party soon.
3  For the time being I'm spending so much of the day
   earning money that I don't have time to become rich.
4  The English are usually having supper at 8.30.
5  English people are always saying sorry.

## A EMPHASISING VERY FREQUENT ACTION

1
2
3
4
5

## B REGULAR ACTION AROUND A POINT OF TIME

| Frequency | Point |
|-----------|-------|
| 1 |  |
| 2 |  |
| 3 |  |
| 4 |  |
| 5 |  |

## C TEMPORARY ACTION FOR A PERIOD

1
2
3
4
5

## D ACTION ONLY AT THE TIME OF SPEAKING

1
2
3
4
5

## E FUTURE ARRANGEMENT

1
2
3
4
5

## NOT SURE?

# Time box bingo sentences

1 This is Peter Snow reporting from London. As I stand here, the rain is pouring down.

2 My husband's wonderful – he's almost always giving me presents.

3 She used to be overweight but nowadays she's eating less.

4 Don't forget to knock hard; I'm often working in the garden at lunchtime.

5 I'm staying at home tomorrow, so come around for tea.

6 The manager is away, I'm afraid. He's currently visiting Japan.

7 Our boss is retiring at the end of the month – he's 65.

8 Sometimes he's resting at this time of the day, so don't ring him now, ring him later.

9 Right now the Prime Minister's walking into the hall.

10 I can't sleep. My neighbour's continually playing loud music.

11 I hate driving in London. I'm forever losing my way.

12 Don't worry, he's coming. He's putting on his hat at this very second.

13 She's normally travelling home about now.

14 At present I'm learning two languages at evening classes.

15 We're not having a holiday next year. It'll be too difficult with the new baby.

16 Hurry up! They're broadcasting the match at this very moment.

17 These days she's working in another department.

18 Look at the rain! Just think, we're generally camping by the sea at this time of year.

19 It's very difficult to do any work, the children are constantly interrupting me.

20 I'm so tired! Thank goodness I'm having a holiday fairly shortly.

# 1.9 – The changing present

1 Nowadays the population in all countries is decreasing. However, the population of the elderly is increasing due to better standards of living.

2 These days many families worldwide are having to restrict how often they eat meat because it is becoming too expensive.

3 The world is currently undergoing a change in climatic conditions. The weather is more difficult to predict and winters are starting later.

4 The English are destroying their own language. At present people are not following traditional grammar rules. For example, the difference between *I shall* and *I will* is disappearing. And *if I was you* is replacing *if I were you*.

5 In many countries jails are full or overcrowded and for the time being the crime rate is going up.

6 For the present young people are following fashion and there is not very much difference in their dress.

7 The Russians and the Americans are being very open about their nuclear policies these days. Other countries are not being so cooperative.

8 Right at this moment 7,000 man-made objects are orbiting the Earth and this number is increasing daily.

9 It is not a good idea to visit countries in the northern hemisphere in October because they are usually having their annual invasion of tourists then.

10 The poor are always accusing the rich of being lazy and badly organised financially.

11 The economy of all countries is booming now and everyone is importing and exporting more than before.

12 At the moment the Brazilian government is controlling the cutting down of the Amazon jungle and the world is not losing its oxygen supply. The Amazon provides a high proportion of the world's oxygen.

13 At the moment the quality of life is improving all over the world.

14 *Romeo and Juliet* has a great plot. One day Romeo is fighting in a war when he suddenly sees a very beautiful girl trying to escape from some soldiers.

# 1.10 – Progress report: Master sheet

| | | |
|---|---|---|
| 1 | **When does the train leave?**<br>**When's the train leaving?** | A Usually at seven.<br>B Any minute now if there are no more delays. |
| 2 | **How often are you playing darts?**<br>**How often do you play darts?** | A Several times a day as long as the competition lasts.<br>B Every now and then. |
| 3 | Why does water boil?<br>Why is the water boiling? | A **Because a physical change takes place.**<br>B **Because the gas is still on.** |
| 4 | Peter tells me your brother's married.<br>Peter's telling me about your brother's marriage. | A **Yes, I saw you talking to Peter a few minutes ago.**<br>B **Well, don't let me interrupt you** |
| 5 | **The Earth travels at 107,000 km per hour.**<br>**The Earth is travelling at 100,000 km**<br>**per hour.** | A Yes, I know. It has always travelled at that speed.<br>B Yes, it's slowing down and scientists can't explain why. |
| 6 | You clock in now, don't you?<br>You're clocking in now, aren't you? | A **Yes, every day at nine.**<br>B **Yes, I'm late.** |
| 7 | Josceline lives in Bristol.<br>Josceline's living in Bristol. | A That's right, she moved there ten years ago.<br>B That's right, she's got a temporary job there. |
| 8 | **How do you do?**<br>**How are you doing?** | A Nice to meet you.<br>B Nicely, thank you. |
| 9 | **Why don't you sit down?**<br>**Why aren't you sitting down?** | A Thank you.<br>B I'm sorry. |
| 10 | He sings whenever I arrive.<br>He's always singing whenever I arrive. | A He's just trying to impress you, I expect.<br>B He's permanently happy, that's all. |
| 11 | You go straight on.<br>You're going straight on. | A **And then?**<br>B **Don't worry, I live just up the road.** |
| 12 | **She speaks two languages, doesn't she?**<br>**She's speaking two languages, isn't she?** | A Yes, she's bilingual.<br>B Yes, she's a bit confused. |
| 13 | The great American athlete is winning.<br>The great American athlete wins. | A **Yes, but he's beginning to slow down.**<br>B **What a victory!** |
| 14 | He's going out whenever I phone.<br>He goes out whenever I phone. | A **Yes, he's very busy these days.**<br>B **Really? I don't think he likes you.** |
| 15 | The neighbours are friendly.<br>The neighbours are being friendly. | A **Yes, it's a friendly neighbourhood.**<br>B **Yes, it makes quite a change.** |
| 16 | Whatever do you talk about?<br>Whatever are you talking about? | A **That's the problem, I find them so boring.**<br>B **This morning's news.** |
| 17 | **What do you weigh?**<br>**What are you weighing?** | A About sixty-seven kilos.<br>B Some parcels to send to Italy. |
| 18 | **I'm coming from Canada.**<br>**I come from Canada.** | A What time does the plane leave Toronto?<br>B Which part of Canada do you live in? |
| 19 | **What do you think?**<br>**What are you thinking?** | A You already know my opinion.<br>B About my future. |
| 20 | **Are you getting a lot of snow?**<br>**Do you get a lot of snow?** | A Yes, we're completely cut off.<br>B Occasionally. |
| 21 | **How often does the postman come?**<br>**How often is the postman coming?** | A Once a day.<br>B Three times a day but only until Christmas. |
| 22 | Where do you have lunch?<br>Where are you having lunch? | A **Usually at home.**<br>B **I haven't decided.** |
| 23 | I'm on a diet at present.<br>I'm a vegetarian. | A **So I suppose you aren't eating bacon.**<br>B **So I suppose you don't eat bacon.** |

# Progress report

| | |
|---|---|
| 1 | A Usually at seven.<br>B Any minute now if there are no more delays. |
| 2 | A Several times a day as long as the competition lasts.<br>B Every now and then. |
| 3 Why does water boil?<br>Why is the water boiling? | A<br>B |
| 4 Peter tells me your brother's married.<br>Peter's telling me about your brother's marriage. | A<br>B |
| 5 | A Yes, I know. It has always travelled at that speed.<br>B Yes, it's slowing down and scientists can't explain why. |
| 6 You clock in now, don't you?<br>You're clocking in now, aren't you? | A<br>B |
| 7 | A That's right, she moved there ten years ago.<br>B That's right, she's got a temporary job there. |
| 8 | A Nice to meet you.<br>B Nicely, thank you. |
| 9 | A Thank you.<br>B I'm sorry. |
| 10 | A He's just trying to impress you, I expect.<br>B He's permanently happy, that's all. |
| 11 You go straight on.<br>You're going straight on. | A<br>B |
| 12 | A Yes she's bilingual.<br>B Yes, she's a bit confused. |
| 13 The great American athlete is winning.<br>The great American athlete wins. | A<br>B |
| 14 He's going out whenever I phone.<br>He goes out whenever I phone. | A<br>B |
| 15 The neighbours are friendly.<br>The neighbours are being friendly. | A<br>B |
| 16 Whatever do you talk about?<br>Whatever are you talking about? | A<br>B |
| 17 | A About sixty-seven kilos.<br>B Some parcels to send to Italy. |
| 18 | A What time does the plane leave Toronto?<br>B Which part of Canada do you live in? |
| 19 | A You already know my opinion.<br>B About my future. |
| 20 | A Yes, we're completely cut off.<br>B Occasionally. |
| 21 | A Once a day.<br>B Three times a day but only until Christmas. |
| 22 Where do you have lunch?<br>Where are you having lunch? | A<br>B |
| 23 I'm on a diet at present.<br>I'm a vegetarian. | A<br>B |

# Progress Report: Jumble

1) Josceline lives in Bristol.

2) He sings whenever I arrive.

3) How often are you playing darts?

4) What are you weighing?

5) How do you do?

6) I'm coming from Canada.

7) The Earth travels at 107,000 km per hour.

8) What are you thinking?

9) So I suppose you don't eat bacon.

10) How often does the postman come?

11) Why don't you sit down?

12) She's speaking 2 languages, isn't she?

13) Are you getting a lot of snow?

14) When does the train leave?

15) Josceline is living in Bristol.

16) She speaks 2 languages, doesn't she?

17) Why aren't you sitting down?

18) The Earth is travelling at 100,000 km per hour.

19) Do you get a lot of snow?

20) When's the train leaving?

21) I come from Canada.

22) How are you doing?

23) How often is the postman coming?

24) What do you think?

25) Because a physical change takes place.

26) Usually at home.

27) Yes, it's a friendly neighbourhood.

28) Yes, it makes quite a change.

29) Yes, I'm late.

30) Yes, he's very busy these days.

31) Well, don't let me interrupt you.

32) I haven't decided.

33) That's the problem, I find them so boring.

34) Yes, every day at 9.

35) And then?

36) But he's beginning to slow down.

37) Really? I don't think he likes you.

38) Don't worry, I live just up the road.

39) What a victory!

40) Because the gas is still on.

41) How often do you play darts?

42) So I suppose you aren't eating bacon.

43) What do you weigh?

44) He's always singing whenever I arrive.

45) This morning's news.

46) Yes, I saw you talking to Peter a few minutes ago.

# 1.11 — Guess who . . .

= BY TRAIN    = BY UNDERGROUND

| DAY 1 | DAY 2 | DAY 3 | DAY 4 | DAY 5 | DAY 1 | DAY 2 | DAY 3 | DAY 4 | DAY 5 | DAY 1 | DAY 2 | DAY 3 | DAY 4 | DAY 5 | DAY 1 | DAY 2 | DAY 3 | DAY 4 | DAY 5 |

TODAY  MAURICE — TODAY  GREG — TODAY  TOM — TODAY  FRED

| DAY 1 | DAY 2 | DAY 3 | DAY 4 | DAY 5 | DAY 1 | DAY 2 | DAY 3 | DAY 4 | DAY 5 | DAY 1 | DAY 2 | DAY 3 | DAY 4 | DAY 5 | DAY 1 | DAY 2 | DAY 3 | DAY 4 | DAY 5 |

| DAY 1 | DAY 2 | DAY 3 | DAY 4 | DAY 5 | DAY 1 | DAY 2 | DAY 3 | DAY 4 | DAY 5 | DAY 1 | DAY 2 | DAY 3 | DAY 4 | DAY 5 | DAY 1 | DAY 2 | DAY 3 | DAY 4 | DAY 5 |

TODAY  MARTIN — TODAY  DENNIS — TODAY  TIM — TODAY  GUY

| DAY 1 | DAY 2 | DAY 3 | DAY 4 | DAY 5 | DAY 1 | DAY 2 | DAY 3 | DAY 4 | DAY 5 | DAY 1 | DAY 2 | DAY 3 | DAY 4 | DAY 5 | DAY 1 | DAY 2 | DAY 3 | DAY 4 | DAY 5 |

| DAY 1 | DAY 2 | DAY 3 | DAY 4 | DAY 5 | DAY 1 | DAY 2 | DAY 3 | DAY 4 | DAY 5 | DAY 1 | DAY 2 | DAY 3 | DAY 4 | DAY 5 | DAY 1 | DAY 2 | DAY 3 | DAY 4 | DAY 5 |

TODAY  EDWARD — TODAY  WILLIAM — TODAY  JONATHAN — TODAY  MATT

| DAY 1 | DAY 2 | DAY 3 | DAY 4 | DAY 5 | DAY 1 | DAY 2 | DAY 3 | DAY 4 | DAY 5 | DAY 1 | DAY 2 | DAY 3 | DAY 4 | DAY 5 | DAY 1 | DAY 2 | DAY 3 | DAY 4 | DAY 5 |

| DAY 1 | DAY 2 | DAY 3 | DAY 4 | DAY 5 | DAY 1 | DAY 2 | DAY 3 | DAY 4 | DAY 5 | DAY 1 | DAY 2 | DAY 3 | DAY 4 | DAY 5 | DAY 1 | DAY 2 | DAY 3 | DAY 4 | DAY 5 |

TODAY  TREVOR — TODAY  JOHN — TODAY  LUKE — TODAY  STEVE

| DAY 1 | DAY 2 | DAY 3 | DAY 4 | DAY 5 | DAY 1 | DAY 2 | DAY 3 | DAY 4 | DAY 5 | DAY 1 | DAY 2 | DAY 3 | DAY 4 | DAY 5 | DAY 1 | DAY 2 | DAY 3 | DAY 4 | DAY 5 |

| DAY 1 | DAY 2 | DAY 3 | DAY 4 | DAY 5 | DAY 1 | DAY 2 | DAY 3 | DAY 4 | DAY 5 | DAY 1 | DAY 2 | DAY 3 | DAY 4 | DAY 5 | DAY 1 | DAY 2 | DAY 3 | DAY 4 | DAY 5 |

TODAY  MIKE — TODAY  RAY — TODAY  TED — TODAY  PAUL

| DAY 1 | DAY 2 | DAY 3 | DAY 4 | DAY 5 | DAY 1 | DAY 2 | DAY 3 | DAY 4 | DAY 5 | DAY 1 | DAY 2 | DAY 3 | DAY 4 | DAY 5 | DAY 1 | DAY 2 | DAY 3 | DAY 4 | DAY 5 |

| DAY 1 | DAY 2 | DAY 3 | DAY 4 | DAY 5 | DAY 1 | DAY 2 | DAY 3 | DAY 4 | DAY 5 | DAY 1 | DAY 2 | DAY 3 | DAY 4 | DAY 5 | DAY 1 | DAY 2 | DAY 3 | DAY 4 | DAY 5 |

TODAY  ARTHUR — TODAY  DAVE — TODAY  PETER — TODAY  CHARLES

| DAY 1 | DAY 2 | DAY 3 | DAY 4 | DAY 5 | DAY 1 | DAY 2 | DAY 3 | DAY 4 | DAY 5 | DAY 1 | DAY 2 | DAY 3 | DAY 4 | DAY 5 | DAY 1 | DAY 2 | DAY 3 | DAY 4 | DAY 5 |

# 1.12 – Perfect Choice

FBI agents believe they have caught the thief who has been stealing from the 1.8 million telephone boxes scattered across the US.

Galling though it is to British Telecom, the standard American pay phone is all but impervious to interference – except by tractor, sledgehammer and a legendary thief called James Clark.

In an eight-year spree Clark, an Ohio machinist and diemaker, aged 48, has accumulated a steady income of over $500,000 from coin boxes in 24 states. Never too greedy and always on the move in his blue Chevy Astro van, Clark stayed ahead of the law – until last week.

But a statement by the FBI's northern Ohio office in Akron – where the suspect is likely to face charges within 10 days – revealed that a man believed to be Clark had been arrested by agents in Los Angeles where he had apparently settled after years on the move.

Clark had lived in small motels, discreetly offloading his store of stolen coins in cheap groceries.

Last year seven local Bell Telephone companies put up a $25,000 reward for his arrest. It was not known yesterday whether the reward would be collected or what kind of lock-picking device Clark used.

A Pacific Bell spokesman said: "We are very pleased to have a suspect in custody. He's been a pain in our phones for a long while."

*THE GUARDIAN*

1 This is about the phone box mystery that have at last been solved.

2 The reports were always the same: 'The thief has just stolen from a coin box and is just gone.'

3 The FBI're been looking for the thief for the last eight years.

4 Have you heard that the police have just had their first bit of luck?

5 They've just arrest the thief.

6 He's been a pain in our phones since a long time.

7 Has been charged James Clark?

8 Now that they have arrested him, they'll probably charge him within ten days.

9 The FBI have waiting many years for this moment.

10 He's with the police since last week.

11 He's never done any stealing except from coin boxes.

12 Clark has been given the telephone companies a lot of trouble.

13 James Clark must wait until the police have been holding him for another ten days before he faces charges.

14 He's been arrested last week.

15 He's been stealing from phones eight years ago.

16 The suspect's address's been discovered by the police

## Substitution table

| Positive | I, you, we, they | (long form) \_\_\_\_\_ | Present Perfect Active |
| | | (contraction) \_\_\_\_\_ | stop\_\_\_Clark. |
| | He, she, (it) | (long form) \_\_\_\_\_ | |
| | | (contraction) \_\_\_\_\_ | |
| Positive question | \_\_\_\_\_ \_\_\_\_\_ | I, you, we, they he, she, (it) | Present Perfect Passive \_\_\_\_\_ arrest\_\_\_ . |
| Negative | (I), you, we, they | (long form) \_\_\_\_\_ | |
| | | (contraction) \_\_\_\_\_ | Present Perfect Continuous |
| | He, she, it | (long form) \_\_\_\_\_ | \_\_\_\_\_ steal\_\_\_ again. |
| | | (contraction) \_\_\_\_\_ | |
| Negative question | (contraction) \_\_\_\_\_ (contraction) \_\_\_\_\_ | (I), you, we, they he, she, it | |
| Tag question | They He | (contraction) \_\_\_\_\_ (contraction) \_\_\_\_\_ | charge \_\_\_ Clark, \_\_\_ \_\_\_? \_\_\_ \_\_\_? |

# Africa braces itself for new plague

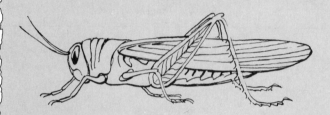

**Tim Radford**
**Science correspondent**

The rains which have just brought hope to the starving in Africa have also triggered a new menace – the biggest plague of locusts in three decades.

Experts who have been with the Food and Agriculture Organisation in Mali for years were amazed by the size of one swarm measuring 75 by 16 miles. Such a swarm could contain 150 billion insects, between them eating 300,000 tons of fresh vegetation every day. And there are other swarms.

Giant swarms have also been reported in Cape Verde and Burkina Faso. In Botswana, according to the FAO, locusts have covered between one and two million acres. There have also been reports of a rapid spread of desert locusts in Guinea, Senegal, Mauritania, and Niger, and in Libya, Egypt and Saudi Arabia.

The last major outbreak of locusts was in 1963. 'There are areas to which they retreat in very dry weather, and enough survive so that once it starts raining and raining widely there is suddenly perhaps a 500 per cent rise in population, through a generation, which takes a month.'

Tunisia, Morocco and Algeria have carried out spraying of both juvenile and adult locusts this year. Other countries are waiting until international meetings have been held in two months' time before making definite plans on how to confront the crisis. However, governments cannot wait until the locust swarms have eaten their crops – that would spell economic disaster.

THE GUARDIAN

1 a) Were the rains recent or a long time ago?
  b) Which adverb can replace *just*?

2 Is their employment with the FAO at an end?

3 When exactly were these reports received?

4 a) Does *have been held* refer to an action in the present, past, or future?
  b) Do we know when the meetings will take place?

5 a) Does *have eaten* refer to an action in the present, past, or future?
  b) Do we know exactly when the locusts will eat the crops?

# 1.14 – Locusts past and present

A Write the uses of the present perfect simple in the table.

| indefinite future period | | indefinite past | |
|---|---|---|---|
| definite future period | | past-present period: unfinished | recent action |

| Example sentence | Use | Timeline |
|---|---|---|
| 1 The rains have just brought hope to the starving in Africa. | | |
| 2 Giant swarms of locusts have been reported in Cape Verde. | | |
| 3 Experts who have been with the FAO in Mali for years were amazed by the size of one swarm. | | |
| 4 Other countries are waiting until international meetings have been held in two months time. | | |
| 5 Governments cannot wait until locust swarms have eaten their crops. | | |

B Draw timelines for examples 1 to 5 in A above.

C 1 a) The rains have just brought hope to the starving in Africa.
   b) The rains just brought hope to the starving but no solution.
   Which adverbs can replace just in a), and in b)?

2 a) Giant swarms of locusts have been reported in Cape Verde.
   b) Giant swarms of locusts were reported in Cape Verde.
   To which sentence can the words *two days ago* be added?

3 a) Experts who have been with the FAO for years were amazed.
   b) Experts who were with the FAO for years were amazed.
   Are the experts still working for the FAO in a), in b)?

4 a) Other countries are waiting until international meetings have been held in two months time.
   b) Other countries are waiting until international meetings are held in two months time.
   Are these countries waiting until the meetings are over or until they begin in a), in b)?

5 a) Other countries are waiting until international meetings have finished.
   b) Other countries are waiting until international meetings finish.
   There is no objective difference between the two sentences.
   True/False?
   Which sentence emphasises the completion of the event?

# 1.15 – Tense moments

B

| | |
|---|---|
| **1** a) I've eaten meat on Friday.<br>   b) I ate meat on Friday. | Which Friday are we talking about? |
| **2** a) I haven't eaten Christmas pudding at Christmas.<br>   b) I didn't eat Christmas pudding at Christmas.<br>   c) I didn't eat Christmas pudding at Christmas as a child. | Which Christmas are we talking about? |
| **3** a) Have you ever made custard?<br>   b) Did you ever make custard? | Which can start a conversation? |
| **4** a) I've never eaten roast beef.<br>   b) I never ate roast beef. | Which refers to the youth of a famous cook and which to a live TV programme with a famous cook? |
| **5** A:  Please show me how to cook Yorkshire pudding.<br>   B:  a)  But you've already cooked Yorkshire pudding as good as mine.<br>       b)  But you already cooked Yorkshire pudding as good as mine. | Which logically follows the request? |
| **6** a) My granny made a lot of mincemeat this Christmas.<br>   b) My granny has made a lot of mincemeat this Christmas. | These both refer to the same Christmas. Which can you use during Christmas and which a very short time after Christmas? |
| **7** a) It's almost liquid – Yes, I've stewed the fruit for three hours.<br>   b) It's almost liquid – Yes, I stewed the fruit for three hours. | When did he start stewing the fruit? |
| **8** a) Granny baked many cakes during her lifetime.<br>   b) Granny's baked many cakes during her lifetime. | Is granny dead or alive? |
| **9** a) He brewed some Darjeeling ...<br>   b) He's brewed some Darjeeling ... | Can you add 'and then he poured it out.' to a) or b)? |

C

Time expressions which can be used for both present perfect and past simple:

|  |
|---|
|  |

When you use the above time references with the present perfect simple and the past simple, there is a change of meaning.     **True/False?**

# 1.16 – Is the time up?

| A | B |
|---|---|
| **1** A: Where's John? It's two pm already! | B: I didn't see him this morning. |
| **2** A: Where's John? It's eleven am already! | B: I haven't seen him this morning. |
| **3** A: 'I never saw a submarine at sea,' | B: said the retired captain. |
| **4** A: 'I've never seen a submarine at sea,' | B: said the serving naval officer. |
| **5** A: David Harvard, the director, has died. | B: He made many great films in his long career. |
| **6** A: David Harvard, the director, is planning to start on his last film. | B: He's made many great films in his long career. |
| **7** A: Many froze to death last winter. | B: And even though it's spring, the number dead is still not certain. |
| **8** A: Many have already frozen to death this winter. | B: And many more may die before it's over. |
| **9** A: Bill Jenkins, the former boxing referee, is with us in the studio. | B: 'Bill, in your long career, did you ever see a knockout in the first round of a match?' |
| **10** A: Bill Jenkins, the boxing referee, is with us in the studio. | B: 'Bill, in your long career, have you ever seen a knockout in the first round of a match?' |
| **11** A: There have been a lot of rumours recently. | B: But they still don't know who's spreading them. |
| **12** A: There were a lot of rumours. | B: But they never discovered who spread them. |
| **13** A: She studied two languages at university. | B: Yes, she was at Cambridge in the sixties. |
| **14:** A: She's studied two languages at university. | B: Yes, but I think she's changing to another course. |
| **15.** A: We've been abroad at Christmas. | B: One year we stayed in Majorca. |
| **16** A: We were abroad at Christmas. | B: We stayed in Majorca. |
| **17** A: I knew your parents for many years. | B: They were the perfect couple. |
| **18** A: I have known your parents for many years. | B: They are the perfect couple. |

# 1.17 – Have you got the right time?

## A

| Time expressions | Definitions |
|---|---|
| 1  ever since | a)  emphatic way of saying *after* |
| 2  just (=recency) | b)  until now |
| 3  yet | c)  a day in the past |
| 4  lately | d)  a past point |
| 5  so far/up to now | e)  emphatic way of saying *since* |
| 6  ever after | f)  very short time before |
| 7  the other day | g)  until now (in questions and the negative) |
| 8  (three weeks) ago | h)  recently (used for repeated action) |

## B

| | |
|---|---|
| yet | so far/up to now |
| lately | ever after |
| ever since | the other day |
| just (=recency) | (three weeks) ago |
| until (yesterday/last year/three days ago) | when (+ past event/state) |
| that (winter/Easter/day) | after (+ past event/state/time) |
| before now | before (+ past event/state/time) |
| until now | since (last night/I was a girl) |
| last (year/month/week) | yesterday |

| Time adverbials connected with past and present. <br> = _____  _____  _____ tense | Time adverbials connected with past only <br> = _____  _____ tense |
|---|---|
| | |

## D

With all the above time adverbials you can use the present perfect simple and the past simple. **True/False?**

# 1.18 – Time sort dominoes

| | | | |
|---|---|---|---|
| I've heard that excuse | until now | I never heard that excuse | since Friday |
| I've missed a lot of trains | yesterday | It was really hot | lately |
| It's been really hot | on Friday | Has she worked here? | until last week |
| Did he come to see you? | before now | I worked here | so far |
| We've only been late once | the other day | I was a vegetarian | yet |
| I've seen that film three times | many years ago | He lost his job | already |
| Have you finished reading the paper? | up to now | I haven't broken any bones | ever since |
| She stayed in bed | just | He's left | all yesterday |
| She's stayed in bed | yet | We haven't run out of petrol | after the accident |

# A perfect match

**1** I've seen that film three times.

**2** He lost his job.

**3** It was really hot.

**4** He's left.

**5** We haven't run out of petrol.

**6** I was a vegetarian.

**7** Have you finished the paper?

| | |
|---|---|
| **A** | many years ago |
| **B** | already |
| **C** | yesterday |
| **D** | lately |
| **E** | all yesterday |
| **F** | yet |
| **G** | ever since |
| **H** | until last week |
| **I** | after the accident |
| **J** | that month |
| **K** | up to now |
| **L** | the other day |
| **M** | since Friday |
| **N** | just (=recently) |
| **O** | on Friday |
| **P** | before now |
| **Q** | until now |
| **R** | so far |
| **S** | last October |

# 1.19 – Townscapes

 **Camford 1986**

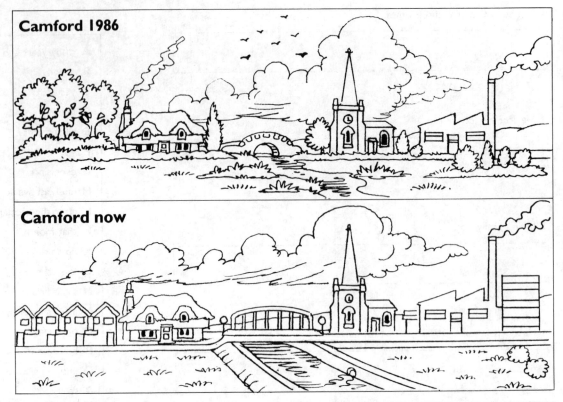

**Camford now**

 **Oxtown 1985**

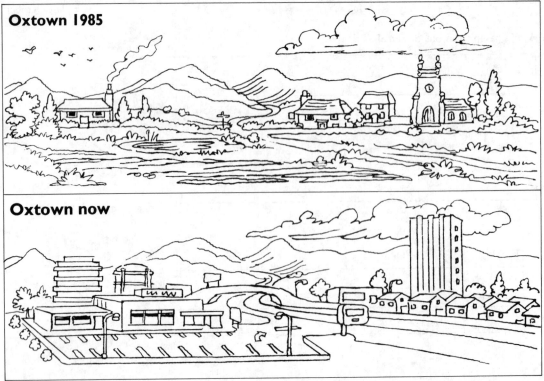

**Oxtown now**

# 1.20 – The search continues

ALBERT:   I've been reading the current issue of *Plant News* and so far I can't see any mention of my research.

BERT:   Well, *I've* read your journal. And I see that you've been working on the same problem *I've* been working on for the last twenty years!

**1**
a)   When did Albert start reading *Plant News*?
b)   Did Albert finish reading all of *Plant News*?
c)   Did Bert finish reading all of the journal?
d)   When did their research begin?
e)   Is their research continuing?
f)   Is their research complete?

ALBERT:   What's that awful smell?

BERT:   I've been making another kind of tea, I'm afraid. It wasn't easy. I think I'll go back to coffee.

**2**
a)   When did Bert finish making his tea?
b)   Is there any evidence of his tea-making?
c)   Is his attempt to make tea finished?
d)   Is the tea-making seen as a process extended in time or as a whole?

ALBERT:   Just think, this greenhouse has been standing here for thirty years and now they want to pull it down.

**3**
a)   When was the greenhouse built?
b)   Is the greenhouse still standing?
c)   Is the existence of the greenhouse *seen* as temporary or permanent?

ALBERT:   Let's wait until we've been working here for a few more years before we tell anyone that we can't remember what we're researching.

**4** Does *a few more years* belong to the past or the future?

**5** The present perfect continuous is used to talk about actions/situations in periods which continue:

a) up to the recent past                          **True/False?**
b) up to the present                              **True/False?**
c) up to the present and into the future          **True/False?**
d) from the present into the future               **True/False?**

# 1.21 – The search has been going on and on and on . . .

**1**
a) I've been reading the current issue of *Plant News*.
b) I've read the current issue of *Plant News*.

i) Has the speaker in a) definitely finished reading *Plant News*?
ii) Has the speaker in b) definitely finished reading *Plant News*?

**2**
a) You've been working on the same problem for the last twenty years.
b) You've worked on the same problem for the last twenty years.

c) I've been making some tea.
d) I've made some tea.

e) Let's wait until we've been working here for a few more years.
f) Let's wait until we've worked here for a few more years.

i) In all these pairs both sentences have the same meaning objectively. **True**/**False**?
ii) In which sentences does the speaker emphasise an ongoing process?

**3**
a) This greenhouse has been standing here for thirty years and now they want to pull it down.
b) This greenhouse has stood here for thirty years.

Which verb form suggests that the situation is permanent – the present perfect simple or the present perfect continuous?

## Summary: Present perfect simple or present perfect continuous?

Would you make any changes to the following summary?
With the use of the present perfect simple or continuous there are two basic issues.

**1** The difference is objectively very clear.

*I've painted the house blue.* (Thank goodness that job's over!)
*I've been painting the house blue.* (I hope to finish it on Monday)

Here the present perfect simple is used for finished actions. The present perfect continuous describes actions which are clearly incomplete.

**2** There is no objective difference when you use a specific time, e.g. *for, since, all my life.*

a) *I've studied the stars for years and I still know very little about the Milky Way.*
*I've been studying the stars for years and I still know very little about the Milky Way.*

b) *I've flown jumbo jets all my life.* (And I can't see myself flying anything else.)
*I've been flying jumbo jets all my life.* (But next week I'm changing my job.)

The differences can only be subjective. In a) the present perfect continuous emphasises the extended period of time and the ongoing process. In b) the present perfect simple sees the situation as permanent whereas the present perfect continuous sees the situation as temporary. So in these contexts you cannot make a grammatical mistake! However, if you want to show a subtle difference, you need to think carefully about the choice between the two verb forms.

# 1.23 – Cassette sales

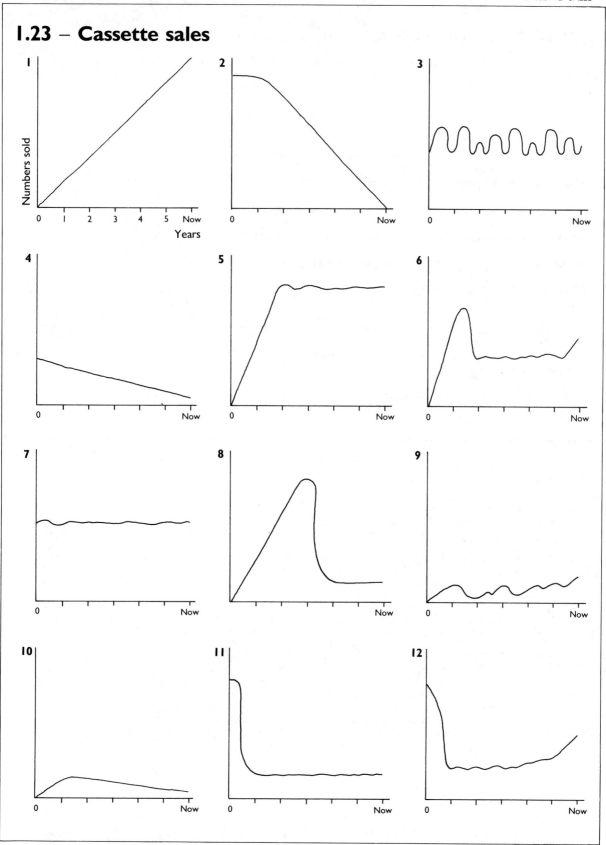

# Trends in cassette sales

a) Sales rose dramatically about six years ago and have remained stable ever since.

b) Sales have not changed for the last six years and are continuing to be stable.

c) Sales fell sharply 6 years ago, have remained stable for the past five years and are increasing slightly now.

d) Sales have risen sharply over the last six years and are continuing to increase.

e) Sales have fallen sharply and consistently over the past five years.

f) Sales have been increasing slightly for six years and are still going up.

g) Sales rose slowly five years ago and have been decreasing slightly ever since.

h) Sales have fluctuated for the last six years and are still going up and down.

i) Sales fell dramatically six years ago and have remained stable ever since; they are continuing to be stable.

j) Sales have slowly decreased for the past six years and are still going down.

k) Sales went up sharply about five years ago; they dropped immediately, remained stable and are now increasing again.

l) Sales went up rapidly five years ago and then decreased sharply; they have been stable ever since.

# 1.24 – Ups and downs

**Part A**

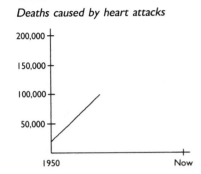

Deaths caused by heart attacks

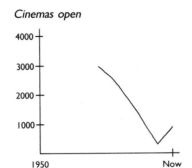

Cinemas open

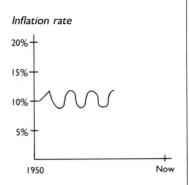

Inflation rate

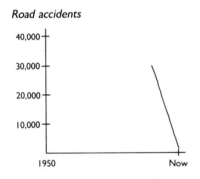

Road accidents

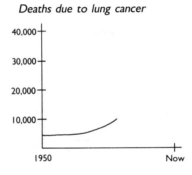

Deaths due to lung cancer

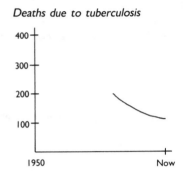

Deaths due to tuberculosis

**Part B**

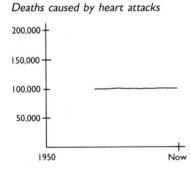

Deaths caused by heart attacks

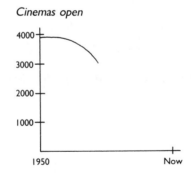

Cinemas open

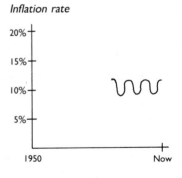

Inflation rate

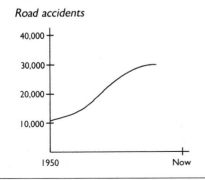

Road accidents

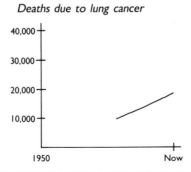

Deaths due to lung cancer

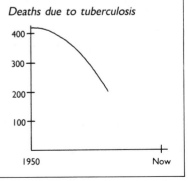

Deaths due to tuberculosis

# 1.25 – Deleted transformations

**1** He's still downstairs.

| _____ | has | _____ | _____ | _____ | _____ . |
|---|---|---|---|---|---|
| 1 | 2 | 3 | 4 | 5 | 6 |

**2** Jean set off for Liverpool a few minutes ago.

| _____ | _____ | _____ | _____ | _____ | _____ | _____ . |
|---|---|---|---|---|---|---|
| 1 | 2 | 3 | 4 | 5 | 6 | 7 |

**3** She hasn't eaten roast beef before.

| _____ | is | _____ | _____ | _____ | _____ | _____ | _____ | _____ | _____ . |
|---|---|---|---|---|---|---|---|---|---|
| 1 | 2 | 3 | 4 | 5 | 6 | 7 | 8 | 9 | 10 |

**4** It's a really long time since we went to the wax museum.

| _____ | have | _____ | _____ | _____ | _____ | _____ | _____ | _____ | _____ . |
|---|---|---|---|---|---|---|---|---|---|
| 1 | 2 | 3 | 4 | 5 | 6 | 7 | 8 | 9 | 10 |

**5** Is this the first time you've needed glasses?

| _____ | you | _____ | _____ | _____ | _____ ? |
|---|---|---|---|---|---|
| 1 | 2 | 3 | 4 | 5 | 6 |

**6** They last went swimming at the beginning of autumn.

| _____ | have | _____ | _____ | _____ | _____ | _____ | _____ | _____ | _____ . |
|---|---|---|---|---|---|---|---|---|---|
| 1 | 2 | 3 | 4 | 5 | 6 | 7 | 8 | 9 | 10 |

**7** I got to the airport an hour ago and there's still no news of my wife's plane.

| _____ | _____ | _____ | _____ | _____ | _____ | wife | _____ | _____ | _____ . |
|---|---|---|---|---|---|---|---|---|---|
| 1 | 2 | 3 | 4 | 5 | 6 | 7 | 8 | 9 | 10 |

**8** I still haven't heard from anybody.

| _____ | has | _____ | _____ | _____ | _____ . |
|---|---|---|---|---|---|
| 1 | 2 | 3 | 4 | 5 | 6 |

**9** We haven't had a thunderstorm for ages.

| _____ | _____ | _____ | _____ | we | _____ | _____ | _____ . |
|---|---|---|---|---|---|---|---|
| 1 | 2 | 3 | 4 | 5 | 6 | 7 | 8 |

**10** They went to Hong Kong last year, the year before that, and the year before that!

| _____ | _____ | _____ | _____ | _____ | _____ | _____ | _____ | _____ | _____ ! |
|---|---|---|---|---|---|---|---|---|---|
| 1 | 2 | 3 | 4 | 5 | 6 | 7 | 8 | 9 | 10 |

# 1.26 – Deadly mistake

**1**
The body is here for three hours. The police arrived ten minutes ago.

**2**
The daughter is here for a week – she arrived yesterday.

**3**
You can't go inside – they take photographs now.

**4**
It's a long time we haven't had a murder like this.

**5**
He's been arguing with his wife before.

**6**
Somebody *came/has come* earlier but nobody was at home.

**7**
This is the first time I *saw/have seen* so much blood.

**8**
A: I *found/have found* the corpse at five.

B: That's nothing unusual. I *have often found/often found* corpses at that time.

**9**
The photographer *hasn't taken/didn't take* any photos yet.

**10**
A: That's a terrible scar on his forehead

B: Yes, he *has cut/cut* himself.

**11**
A: Don't go near the body.

B: But I don't go near it

**12**
I've checked the fingerprints with our records immediately after I've taken them.

**13**
A: The body is very tanned.

B: Yes, he's gone on holiday.

**14**
They have this apartment since 1987.

**15**
*Nobody/somebody* has ever seen such a terrible crime.

**16**
Are you sure the body has been here since three hours?

**17**
The neighbour I spoke to yesterday knew nothing of their marital problems.

**18**
*Has he lost/did he lose* a lot of blood?

**19**
Apparently somebody heard his wife saying to him: 'I've been looking for you all week because I want some money for that vase you *broke/have broken*.'

**20**
A: What have you found?

B: A gun.

A: *Have you ever used* one/*did you ever use* one?

# 2.1 – Fruit machine: Is it a mistake?

| | | |
|---|---|---|
| **1** | London's population not increased from 1955 to 1988. | The population no increased. |
| **2** | It did not happen. | It didn't happen. |
| **3** | In the 1900 Olympics Alvin Kraenzlein cames first in four athletics events. | He come first in four events. |
| **4** | She didn't liked it. | She didn't likes it. |
| **5** | Why did they bought it? | Why they bought it? |
| **6** | He felt down the stairs two minutes ago. | He fallen down the stairs two minutes ago. |
| **7** | She fell happy yesterday. | She felt happy yesterday. |
| **8** | The English football team, Nottingham Forest, was once won forty-two matches in a row. | Nottingham Forest once won forty-two matches in a row. |
| **9** | Who you told? | Who told you? |
| **10** | In 1983 Peter Dowdeswell ate ninety-one metres of spaghetti, didn't he? | He ate it in 1983, wasn't it? |
| **11** | You did this. | You did this? |
| **12** | I dreamed that the past of *dream* is *dreamt*. | A Norwegian laid on a bed of nails for 274 hours in 1984. |
| **13** | Who did you see at the party? | Who didn't you see at the party? |
| **14** | An American did walk around the world in four years. | An American did do it. |
| **15** | Did I not tell you? | Didn't I tell you? |
| **16** | He didn't know why they didn't come. | He didn't know why didn't they come. |
| **17** | In Queensland, Australia, thirty-five policemen travelled over 500 metres on one motorbike. | In Toronto, Terry McGaurant prefered to ride his motorbike solo up the 1760 steps of the 550 metre high Canadian National Tower. |
| **18** | ABC broadcast the 1984 Olympics to 2,500 million people worldwide. | Alaska State Museum once payed £34,750 for a hat. |

# 2.2 – Past a joke

Arthur Ferguson sold things which were not his. In 1923 he sold Trafalgar Square to a rich American for £6,000. In the same year he sold Big Ben for £1,000 and he accepted a down payment of £2,000 for Buckingham Palace. Ferguson was finally caught when trying to sell the Statue of Liberty for $100,000.

**1** a)  In the first sentence *sold* refers to *one action/ several actions*?

   b)  In the second sentence *sold* refers to *one action/several actions*?

   c)  In both sentences *sold* refers to *complete/incomplete actions*?

In 1974 French tight rope walker, Philippe Petit, both delighted and terrified passers-by in New York. Seven times he crossed and re-crossed a 140 foot long wire stretched between the towers of the World Trade Centre – then the world's tallest building. Eventually when he came down, he was arrested.

**2** a)  *delighted* and *terrified* refer to actions which happened *at the same time/one after the other*?

   b)  *came down* and *was arrested* refer to actions which happened *at the same time/one after the other*?

"Excuse me. I wanted to ask you a favour – I wondered if you could give me a push?"

**3** a)  *wanted* and *wondered* refer to the *present/the past/the future*?

   b)  Put the following in order of politeness with the most polite last:

   *I wonder if you could help me . . .*  ☐

   *Could you help me?*  ☐

   *I wondered if you could help me . . .*  ☐

"I'd rather we got married."

**4** a)  *I'd* is short for _____

   b)  *'we got married'* refers to *the present/the past/the future*?

   c)  He is *expressing a preference/talking about the past*?

   d)  *rather* can be replaced with *so __ __ __ r.*

# 2.2 – Past a Joke 2

"I wish we had more than two worms!"

**5** a) How many worms have they got?

b) Do they want more?

c) *Had* refers to *the present/the past/the future?*

"It's high time you took that dog for a PROPER walk!"

**6** a) *took* refers to *the present/the past/the future?*

b) Is the dog usually taken for a proper walk?

c) Why is *high* used here?

## Summary of The Past Simple: true or false?

| The past simple can be used to: | |
|---|---|
| describe completed actions. | **True/False?** |
| describe one finished action. | **True/False?** |
| describe a repeated action. | **True/False?** |
| describe simultaneous actions. | **True/False?** |
| describe actions which happened in sequence. | **True/False?** |
| make a polite request. | **True/False?** |
| express a preference. | **True/False?** |
| express a strong wish. | **True/False?** |
| express a strong recommendation. | **True/False?** |
| talk about the present. | **True/False?** |
| talk about the future. | **True/False?** |
| 'The past simple' is a bad name for the past simple. | **True/False?** |

# 2.4 – Volley ball

| Set A | Set B | Set C | Set D |
|---|---|---|---|
| 1 buy | 1 bear | 1 break | 1 begin |
| 2 cost | 2 bind | 2 bring | 2 beat |
| 3 draw | 3 build | 3 catch | 3 bend |
| 4 fall | 4 deal | 4 choose | 4 bite |
| 5 fight | 5 dig | 5 cut | 5 blow |
| 6 fly | 6 drink | 6 drive | 6 eat |
| 7 forecast | 7 find | 7 freeze | 7 hit |
| 8 grind | 8 flee | 8 grow | 8 know |
| 9 hang | 9 forget | 9 lose | 9 lean |
| 10 hide | 10 lay | 10 ring | 10 learn |
| 11 kneel | 11 lead | 11 sell | 11 mow |
| 12 leap | 12 let | 12 set | 12 ride |
| 13 leave | 13 put | 13 shrink | 13 rise |
| 14 light | 14 read | 14 sing | 14 send |
| 15 make | 15 say | 15 sink | 15 show |
| 16 meet | 16 shoot | 16 spell | 16 shut |
| 17 pay | 17 shake | 17 steal | 17 spell |
| 18 shed | 18 sit | 18 swell | 18 spend |
| 19 slide | 19 speak | 19 take | 19 stick |
| 20 slit | 20 spill | 20 tell | 20 stride |
| 21 sow | 21 swear | 21 throw | 21 strike |
| 22 sting | 22 tear | 22 tread | 22 swim |
| 23 swing | 23 wake | 23 weave | 23 think |
| 24 win | 24 wind | 24 write | 24 teach |

# 2.5 – Who was Jack the Ripper?

Nobody knows the answer but a good detective should be able to find the 'grammar crimes' in the past continuous:

1 Around three o'clock on the night of August 31st 1888, Polly Nichols was
2 being followed through the dark streets and alleys of the East of London
3 by the legendary Jack the Ripper.
4   As Jack the Ripper was killing his first victim, the rest of London
5 was sleeping peacefully. In fact the police was patroling the street of
6 the murder, Buck's Row, half an hour before the body was found by two
7 market porters. They're examining the body to see if it was drunk or
8 dead, when they decided to look for a policeman. When Polly's body was
9 discovered, she wasn't wearing good quality clothes, so the police knew
10 they weren't looking for a thief. There was another mystery. Why she wasn't
11 living with her husband and children at the time of the murder nobody
12 seemed to know. Around the time of the second and third murders,
13 both of which happened very early on Sunday 30th September 1888,
14 some people were sing and dance in the nearby streets. Was not the
15 murderer killing for pleasure or he was killing for some other strange
16 and horrible reason? It is obvious that after three brutal murders, the
17 residents were becoming extremely frightened. In fact the Ripper was
18 being so vicious that after the fourth one most people wouldn't go out
19 late at night. Many people investigated the murders and one theory
20 was that Jack the Ripper was a member of the Royal Family.
21   Were hiding some of the evidence the police? That is also a theory
22 never completely forgotten.

## Substitution table

|  | Past continuous |
|---|---|
| **Positive** | Last night I _____ r_____ about Jack the Ripper.<br>On a dark night in 1888 he _____ f_____ Polly Nichols through the streets of London.<br>The police _____ p_____ the streets thirty minutes before the murder. |
| **Negative**<br>**Negative contraction** | They _____ _____ l_____ for a thief.<br>_____ |
| **Questions:**<br>**Positive** | Why _____ y_____ r_____ about Jack the Ripper? |
| **Negative** | Why _____ the police l_____ for a thief? |
| **Tag** | Jack the Ripper _____ k_____ for some strange reason, _____ _____? |
| **Passive** | Polly _____ _____ f_____ through the London streets. |

# 2.6 – Continuous contexts

The arrival of a policeman **interrupted** a thief's attempt to rob a jeweller's shop. The policeman arrived **when the thief was in the middle of throwing** a brick at the window. He claimed the jeweller's was not his target.

A   'Honestly, Constable, I _____
    1

_____ at the _____
    2              3

alarm when _____ _____
                4        5

along.'

---

# The World divorce record holder

In December 1978, 71 year old Glynn de Moss Wolfe made plans to marry for the twenty-second and last time. Till then **he had made a habit of divorcing** his wives.

B   _____ _____ always
     1        2

_____ _____ until _____
   3        4              5

_____ _____ twenty-second
   6        7

_____ , Eva.
   8

---

In rather difficult circumstances Smithers's boss **inquired very carefully and very politely** about a certain office key.

C   '_____ me, Mr Smithers,
      1

_____ _____ w_____
   2        3          4

whether _____ _____
            5        6

_____ _____ where you put
   7        8

the key to the office tea

cupboard.'

In the USA a woman reported the theft of her purse to the manager of a department store. Back at home she received a telephone call to say that she could collect her purse as someone had handed it in. However, **burglars used the time she was on her way to the store to break into her house.**

**D** While she ___ ___ ___
                   1    2    3

___ ___ department store, ___
4    5                    6

___ ___ her ___ .
7    8       9

**It was the middle of the afternoon in an Australian summer. Henry Bourse was in the process of doing some underwater filming.** After an hour of filming he met a shark and lost his leg!

However, Henry was not in the least worried and carried on with his work. Why?!

**E** At three on a summer afternoon Henry Bourse

___ ___ ___ ___
1    2    3    4

Melbourne.

After some time a shark suddenly bit off his leg and

swam away with it. Henry continued filming. ___
                                        5

leg ___ ___ . Another shark ___
    6    7                       8

___ ___ his other leg several years earlier.
9    10

# The least successful target practice

One of the worst misses in military history **occurred during a three week training session** in Portsmouth. The incident involved a destroyer ship and its crew and a tugboat.

**F** In 1947 the crew of the destroyer, HMS Saintes

___ ___ ___ ___ ___
1    2    3    4    5

___ Portsmouth. Their task was to fire at a
6

target pulled by the tugboat, Buccaneer. They fired,

___ the target and ___ the tugboat!
7                    8

# 2.7 – Continuous continued

A    Write the uses of the past continuous in the correct places in the chart.

| emphasising very frequent action | simultaneous actions | action in progress for a period |
|---|---|---|

| action in progress around a point of time | polite tentative request | interrupted action |
|---|---|---|

| Example sentence | Use | Timeline |
|---|---|---|
| **I** Excuse me, I was wondering whether you could tell me where the key is. | | |
| **2** At three he was filming underwater near Melbourne. | | |
| **3** In 1947 the crew were training for three weeks in Portsmouth. | | |
| **4** I was aiming at the fire alarm when you came along. | | |
| **5** He was always getting divorced until he met Eva. | | |
| **6** While she was returning to the store, thieves were burgling her hourse. | | |

B    Now draw the timelines for the sentences in the chart above.

## C    Contrasting past continuous and past simple

**I**
a) Escuse me, I wondered whether you could tell me where the key is.
b) Excuse me, I was wondering whether you could tell me where the key is.

i) Which word can replace *whether*?
ii) Which is more polite/tentative, a) or b)?

**2**
a) At three he was filming a shark underwater.
b) At three he filmed a shark underwater.

Did he start filming before or at three o'clock in a), and in b)?

**3**
a) In 1947 they trained for three weeks in Portsmouth.
b) In 1947 they were training for three weeks in Portsmouth.

One of these tenses is frequently used to begin a story or give the background to a story. Which tense?

**4**
a) I was aiming at the fire alarm when the police came along.
b) I aimed at the fire alarm when the police came along.

What happened first in a) and in b)? Did the police interrupt him in a) or in b)?

**5**
a) He was always having marital problems until he met Eva.
b) He always had marital problems until he met Eva.

Which has more emphasis, a) or b)?

**6**
a) While she returned to the store, thieves burgled her house.
b) While she was returning to the store, thieves were burgling her house.

Which emphasises the duration of the actions, a) or b)?

# 2.8 – Sea saga: Part A

Read the story and number the pictures in the correct sequence.

It was a cold and windy morning in early February 1963 and we were enjoying a four month cruise on the S.S. Southern Cross. We were about to cross the Bay of Biscay on our way to Southampton. It was seven o'clock and I was running upstairs to the next deck, when the captain suddenly raced past me in his pyjamas making for the bridge. At the same time I noticed that the ship was slowly turning around in the direction we had just come from. (Either that or the coast of France was moving.) I decided against going on up to the dining-room for breakfast and went instead to investigate.

The ship was now alive with activity. Alarm bells rang and the next minute sailors tried desperately to lower a lifeboat. It jammed. They tried another but it jammed, too. This did not surprise me as they were always having problems with the boats. By now hundreds of passengers had lined the decks, like the captain many of them still in their pyjamas.

I forced my way to the railings to get a better view. A lifeboat had managed to get free and was on its way towards a figure in the water. Incredible though it was, the crew could hardly row! The figure in the waves was now struggling for his life. All about me there was a mixture of excitement and fear.

The rowers had made slow progress due to their poor training and inexperience and the figure drifted away faster than the crew could row. Then with horror I realised who it was . . . I must have stayed on deck for over an hour; I couldn't move for shock. Suddenly a hand touched my shoulder. A calm but firm voice said, 'Excuse me, sir, but we were wondering whether you could help us with our enquiries into the drowning of your cabin mate.'

## True or False?

1  The ship was in the middle of a four month cruise. **True/False?**
2  The ship was in the process of crossing the Bay of Biscay. **True/False?**
3  The writer saw the captain on his way up the stairs. **True/False?**
4  First alarms rang and then sailors tried to lower a boat into the water. **True/False?**
5  The crew had had problems with the boats on several occasions. **True/False?**
6  The writer was asked very politely to help with enquiries into the drowning. **True/False?**

# Sea saga: Part B

Read the story and number the pictures in the correct sequence.

 a

 b

 c

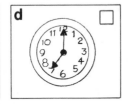 d

 e

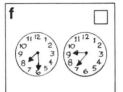 f

 g

 h

 i

 j

 k

 l

 m

We had enjoyed four months of our cruise on the S.S. Southern Cross. It was seven o'clock on a cold and windy morning in February 1963 and we were steaming across the Bay of Biscay en route for Southampton. I ran upstairs to the next deck where I saw the captain in his pyjamas heading for the bridge. Instead of sailing north, the ship was turning slowly around in the direction we had just come from. (Either that or the coast of France was moving.) I was on my way to the dining-room for breakfast but I decided to investigate the situation instead.

The ship was now alive with activity. Alarm bells were ringing and sailors were trying desperately to lower a lifeboat. The boat jammed. They tried another which started to descend but jammed as it was nearing the water. This surprised me as they had only had one previous problem with the boats. By now hundreds of passengers had crowded onto the decks, like the captain many of them still in their pyjamas.

As I watched, all around me there was a mixture of fear and excitement. I forced my way to the railings to get a better view. A lifeboat had managed to get free and made its way to a figure in the water. The figure was now struggling for its life. The crew was rather slow and the figure drifted away from us faster than they could row. Then with horror I realised who the figure was. I must have stayed on deck for over an hour; I could not move for shock. Suddenly somebody touched me on the shoulder. A calm but firm voice said, 'Mr Booth, we want to ask you one or two questions in connection with the drowning of your cabin mate.'

## True or false?

1 The ship was in the middle of a four month cruise.        **True/False?**
2 The ship was in the process of crossing the Bay of        **True/False?**
  Biscay.
3 The writer saw the captain on his way up the stairs.      **True/False?**
4 First alarms rang and then sailors tried to lower a       **True/False?**
  boat into the water.
5 The crew had had problems with the boats on several  **True/False?**
  occasions.
6 The writer was asked very politely to help with          **True/False?**
  enquiries into the drowning.

# 2.9 – Assam: Perfect tea – Is it a thing of the past?

**A1** They had already throw in the tea leaves when they realised I needed warming first.

**A2** Had been you expecting the water to be so hot when they poured it in?

**A3** They waited until the tea had brewing for ten minutes before somebody poured it out.

**A4** They'd used old tea leaves, they'd used stale water instead of fresh, and they hadn't poured the water from the kettle as soon as it had boiled – so of course the tea was undrinkable!

**B1** I had been sleep for a few minutes before I noticed the hot water pouring in.

**B2** Why they had forgotten to warm the pot before putting in the tea leaves?

**B3** Your tea had been left for too long before they poured it out, didn't it?

**B4** They'd not put enough leaves in, so the tea was too weak.

**B5** Why hadn't been made the tea properly?

## Substitution tables

|  | Past perfect simple |
|---|---|
| **Positive** | I _____ m_____ the tea before the water was hot enough. |
| **Positive contraction** | _____ |
| **Negative** | He _____ _____ w_____ the pot before he put in the tea leaves. |
| **Negative contraction** | _____ |
| **Question:** **Positive** | Why _____ y_____ m_____ the tea before the water boiled? |
| **Negative contraction** | _____ y_____ m_____ |
| **Tag** | They _____ m_____ the tea before the water boiled, _____ _____? |
| **Passive** | The tea _____ _____ m_____ before the water boiled. |
| **Passive question** | Why _____ the tea _____ m_____ ? |

|  | Past perfect continuous |
|---|---|
| **Positive** | She _____ _____ m_____ tea for twenty years before Emma told her about warming the pot. |
| **Positive contraction** | _____ |
| **Negative** | We _____ _____ _____ m_____ tea in the afternoon until Emma came to stay. |
| **Negative contraction** | _____ |
| **Question:** **Positive** | How long _____ y_____ _____ m_____ tea before Emma told you about warming the pot? |
| **Negative** | Why _____ y_____ _____ m_____ tea properly before Emma came to stay? |
| **Tag** | We _____ _____ m_____ tea for twenty years before Emma told us about warming the pot, _____ _____? |

# 2.10 – Penalty shot: Sheet A

## Penalty shot

Goalkeeper Pierre Vannier was sure that he would not be re-selected for his local football team in Ferney, near the French-Swiss border. He had made only one successful save that season. However, this was soon to change.

Pierre had left home for a stroll at three in the afternoon on January 5th 1984. He had been out for only five minutes, when the opportunity for him to make the save of his life presented itself. He had rounded the corner into the Avenue des Alpes when he heard a child's screams. Looking up, he was just in time to see five-year-old Marie-Jeanne Musi falling from a fifth floor window. Instinctively, he threw out his arms and caught her.

'It was like saving a hard penalty shot,' said M. Vannier. 'It was a shot I couldn't afford to miss,' he added modestly.

For further news, Pierre and the young girl's shocked parents had to wait until the ambulance arrived and took her to hospital. Marie-Jeanne had nothing worse than a broken arm! For news of his place in the team, Pierre had to wait for a week until his team manager and trainer had discussed his selection. To his delight, his place in the team was assured!

*The Book of Narrow Escapes*

B   Underline all the examples of the past perfect simple in the story.

Now answer these questions.

1 a)  Do we know exactly when Pierre made his one successful save?
   b)  Did he make the save before or after the events in this story?
   c)  Was the season finished?

2  Do we know exactly when he left home for a walk?

3  How long after the start of his walk did he have the chance to save the girl?

4  Did he hear the child's screams before or after he turned the corner?

C   | action at an indefinite point of time |   | action/state through a period |   | action at a definite time |

| Example sentence | Use | Timeline |
|---|---|---|
| 1  He had made only one successful save that season. | | |
| 2  Pierre had left home for a stroll at three in the afternoon on January 5th 1984. | | |
| 3  He had been out for only five minutes, when the opportunity for him to make the save of his life presented itself. | | |

The Past Perfect Simple is used to show clearly that an action or situation happened before another action in the past.     **True/False?**

D   Now draw timelines for the three sentences above in the chart.

# Penalty shot: Sheet B

E | Comparing the past simple and the past perfect simple

Here are some statements in the past simple about the story of 'Penalty shot'.
Are they *True, False,* or is there *No Information* given in the story?

1 Pierre Vannier saved only one goal in the 1983/1984 football season.  **True/False/No information?**
2 Pierre went out for a walk at three pm on January 5th 1984.  **True/False/No information?**
3 Pierre strolled about for five minutes when he heard the girl's screams.  **True/False/No information?**
4 Pierre turned the corner when he heard the screams.  **True/False/No information?**

Put a tick (√) if these statements are correct or a cross (×) if they are incorrect.

a) The past simple can always be used instead of the past perfect simple without changing the meaning.
b) The past simple can sometimes be used instead of the past perfect simple without changing the meaning.
c) The past simple used instead of the past perfect simple changes the meaning of a sentence with *when.*

F | **Summary table**

Put a tick (√) in the appropriate column if the statement is true of the example sentences
and a cross (×) if it is not true.

'Age before beauty': **Past perfect simple before past simple**
If there are two actions in the past, the past perfect simple can be used for the first action in the sequence.

'There is no smoke without fire': **There is no past perfect simple without a past simple**
When a verb is in the past perfect simple, there will always be another verb linked with it in the past simple in the same time period and in the same text (although not necessarily in the same sentence).

'A rose by any other name smells as sweet': The past simple can sometimes be used in place of the past perfect simple without a change of meaning.

| | | | |
|---|---|---|---|
| Pierre had saved only one goal that season. However, this was soon to change. | | | |
| Pierre had left home for a stroll at three ... he heard screams. | | | |
| Pierre had strolled about for five minutes when he heard screams. | | | |
| He had turned the corner when he heard screams.. | | | |

# 2.11 – Romeo, Romeo, ohhh …

It was Kenneth Burke's second wedding day. His new girlfriend, Diana made him wait two years before agreeing to be his second wife.

They were married at the church at eleven and the wedding reception was at twelve in their sixth floor flat in Philadelphia, USA. They were having photographs taken with their guests and went out onto the balcony. They posed for a group photograph and immediately after the camera flash, the groom lost his balance. He grabbed hold of his bride and sent them both toppling to the ground below. Their guests watched in horror and waited for the couple to reach the ground. The newlyweds landed on a patch of rain-softened grass and lived – hopefully happily ever after!

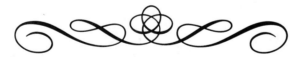

# 2.12 – Flashback

## The least alert burglar

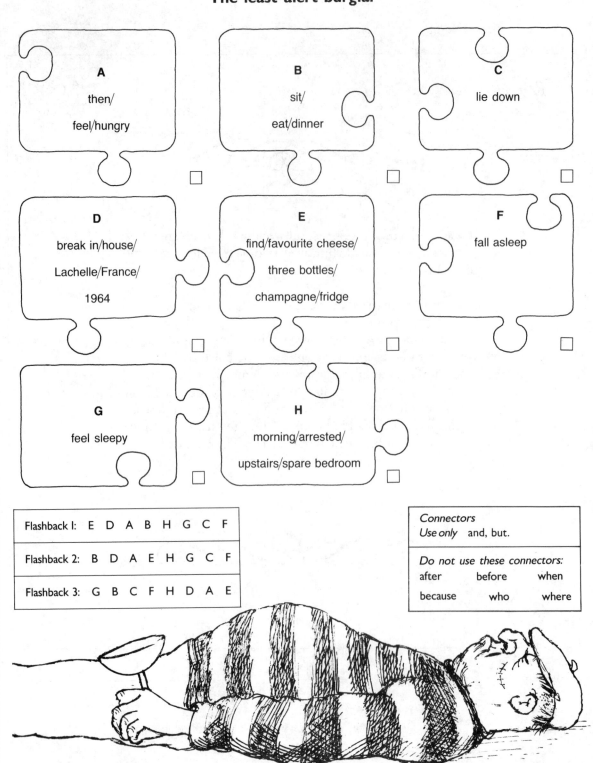

**A**

then/

feel/hungry

☐

**B**

sit/

eat/dinner

☐

**C**

lie down

☐

**D**

break in/house/

Lachelle/France/

1964

☐

**E**

find/favourite cheese/

three bottles/

champagne/fridge

☐

**F**

fall asleep

☐

**G**

feel sleepy

☐

**H**

morning/arrested/

upstairs/spare bedroom

☐

| Flashback I: | E D A B H G C F |
|---|---|
| Flashback 2: | B D A E H G C F |
| Flashback 3: | G B C F H D A E |

**Connectors**
*Use only* and, but.

*Do not use these connectors:*
after          before          when
because          who          where

# 2.13 – The perfect detective

## Who shot Lord Michael Chomley?

Lord Chomley was shot at about eleven pm at his country house one fateful night in July.

Lord and Lady Chomley had sat down to dine with eleven guests at nine. About two hours later shots were heard and Lord Chomley's body was discovered in the library. Some guests had already left by this time.

Detective Inspector Peter Piers-Simple, known as 'The perfect detective', was called to the scene and ordered that any guest who had left the house should be brought back for questioning. Piers-Simple soon realised that five of the guests had plotted the murder together. The five were so nervous that they contradicted themselves. Here are some extracts from what the Chomleys' guests said when interviewed. Read what they said and find the five guilty parties.

**Sir John Hall**

> The murder happened after I left . . . The murder happened after I'd left the house.

**Lady Isobel Bart**

> Lord Chomley was shot before I left . . . Lord Chomley had been murdered before I left for home.

**Lady Chomley**

> My husband shot himself because I left in a terrible temper. . . . He shot himself because I'd walked off in a terrible temper.

**Andrew Rich, the Chomleys' neighbour**

> I heard three shots although I left at eleven. . . . I heard three shots although I'd left at eleven.

**Lord Aston**

> The murder happened when I'd left . . . The murder was committed when I left Lord Chomley's house.

**Elena Richby**

> The shooting took place as soon as I left . . . The shots were fired as soon as I'd left.

**The Duchess of Crewe**

> The terrible act had happened when I left . . . The murder happened at eleven, when I left . . .

**Frederick Baker**

> The murder happened at around eleven, so I left. I couldn't bear to stay in the house . . . The murder had happened at around eleven, so I left.

**Prince John**

> The murder happened at eleven. I left and drove home . . . The murder happened at eleven. I'd left and driven home.

**Lieutenant Tenant**

> Obviously somebody murdered Lord Chomley once I left the house. . . . Obviously somebody murdered Lord Chomley once I'd left the house.

**Sheila Baker**

> The murder took place at eleven but I left; I was drunk, you see . . . The murder happened at eleven but I'd left; I was blind drunk.

**Colonel Kernel**

> He was shot at eleven and I left. I felt terrible . . . He died at eleven and I'd left. I was feeling awful.

## Summary: Connectors and the past simple

**A** Some connectors are logical and so show sequence clearly.
Read the testimonies and list these seven connectors below:

1 _____   2 _____   3 _____

4 _____   5 _____   6 _____

7 _____

After these connectors:

a) both the past perfect simple and the past simple can be used.          **True/False?**

b) the past perfect simple changes the sequence.                         **True/False?**

c) the past perfect simple emphasises which action happened first.        **True/False?**

**B** Some connectors do not show sequence clearly.
Read the testimonies and list these three connectors below:

1 _____   2 _____   3 _____

After these connectors:

a) both the past perfect simple and the past simple can be used.          **True/False?**

b) the past perfect simple changes the sequence.                         **True/False?**

# 2.14 – Antarctica outside, Atlantis inside

I had just been thinking about the terrible winter of 1987, when I saw this advertisement:

## Antarctica outside
## Atlantis inside

The stranger lurked in the doorway of the empty house. Waiting.

The night of January 12, 1987 was one of the coldest in living memory.

Jerry Hibert of East Sheen had been working late in his animation studio and it was 10.30 before he got home. In fact, he had been staying late at work for weeks.

But the sight that greeted him on this particular night when he arrived home was enough to make anyone animated. A mains pipe in the attic had burst and water had been cascading through his house since lunchtime.

Icicles five feet long hung from the roof; the walls were coated in sheets of ice.

But if it was Antarctica outside, it was Atlantis inside.

Water poured down the walls and streamed from the ceiling. Pictures and lamps had been swept aside; furniture and carpets were soaked.

And the dining-room ceiling was now on the dining-room floor.

By the time an emergency plumber had arrived and turned off the mains, Jerry Hibert had had enough. He locked up his sodden home and went to stay with friends.

But while he was settling between the sheets, London was settling under a blanket.

Of snow. So much snow that by morning the city had virtually ground to a halt.

It had been snowing for about twelve hours before he decided to call his insurance company. They said they would send someone as soon as possible.

After saying goodbye to his friends, Mr Hibert set out on the cold journey home.

He wasn't the first to arrive.

Waiting in the doorway was a stranger. The man from Commercial Union.

Because at Commercial Union we don't like to keep our clients waiting. Ever.

We won't make a drama out of a crisis.

a) The writer thought about the winter of 1987. ☐

b) The writer saw the article. ☐

c) Jerry started work. ☐

d) Jerry finished work. ☐

e) Jerry arrived home. ☐

f) The clock struck half past ten. ☐

g) The pipe burst. ☐

h) The water started pouring through the house. ☐

i) The water stopped. ☐

j) It started to snow. ☐

k) It stopped snowing. ☐

l) Jerry started waiting for a change in the weather. ☐

m) Jerry called his insurance company. ☐

n) Jerry arrived home. ☐

o) The insurance man arrived at Jerry's house. ☐

p) Jerry started the habit of working late. ☐

> **Note:**
>
> 1 = the event most distant in the past
>
> 16 = the most recent event

# 2.15 – Practice makes perfect

**A** Help out this student with the questions about the past perfect continuous. Refer to the examples in the text in the previous activity (2.14) to help you.

| | | Right? Wrong? Or what is the answer? |
|---|---|---|
| 1 | How many different uses of this tense are there? — I'm not sure if there are three or four . . . | |
| 2 | Is it used to talk about a finished or an unfinished activity? — A finished activity. | |
| 3 | Can it be used to talk about a habit? — Of course not. | |
| 4 | But isn't this sentence possible: 'I'd been eating a big breakfast for months when my wife suggested dieting.'? — Erm, perhaps it is. | |
| | And what about: 'I'd been eating a really big breakfast when my wife suggested a diet.'? — I think it sounds alright . . . | |
| | How are they different, then? — They mean the same. | |
| 5 | Can the past perfect continuous be used alone without another past tense related to it? — Yes, of course. | |
| | So, can we say, 'Yesterday it had been raining but today it is dry.'? — Yes, I think so. | |
| | Is this correct? 'Yesterday it'd been snowing but today it rained.' — Yes! | |
| 6 | Is the tense used to talk about an action at an indefinite or a definite time in the past? — Both are possible! | |

**B** Write the uses of the Past Perfect Continuous in the table.    **C** Complete timelines for them.

action completed shortly before another      action extending over a past period

action repeated in a past period

| Example sentence | Use | Timeline |
|---|---|---|
| a) I had just been thinking about the terrible winter of 1987 when I saw this advertisement. | | |
| b) He had been staying late at work for weeks. | | |
| c) Water had been cascading through his house since lunchtime. | | |

# 2.17 – Man-eating shark

Rescued after drifting for 118 days in a rubber raft in the middle of the Pacific, Mr Maurice Bailey and his wife could not believe their luck. How they stayed alive was a miracle.

Small sharks, about three feet long, kept swimming up and pushing against the raft. His wife pulled them out by their tails and Maurice wrapped a cloth around their heads until they suffocated. Then they ate them.

The Baileys had sailed from Southampton in June 1972 in their 31ft yacht, *Aurelyn*, bound for New Zealand. One day, halfway between Mexico and the Galapagos Islands, their lunch was scarcely cleared away when the boat was hit by a whale. They watched the water pour into the yacht for an hour before taking to their raft.

They were picked up by a Korean trawler four months later, remarkably fit on a diet of rainwater, raw shark meat, seagulls and the occasional turtle they caught along the way.

# 2.18 – Union Jacks

Which flags contain mistakes in the use of past tenses?

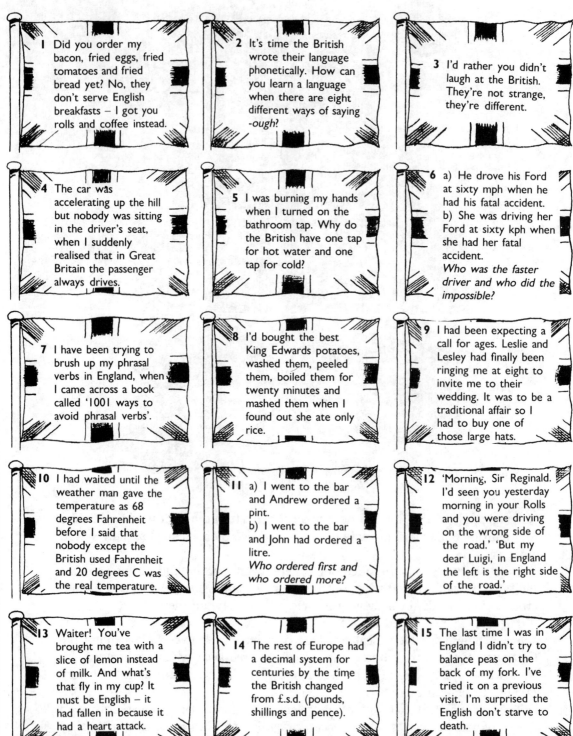

**1** Did you order my bacon, fried eggs, fried tomatoes and fried bread yet? No, they don't serve English breakfasts – I got you rolls and coffee instead.

**2** It's time the British wrote their language phonetically. How can you learn a language when there are eight different ways of saying -ough?

**3** I'd rather you didn't laugh at the British. They're not strange, they're different.

**4** The car was accelerating up the hill but nobody was sitting in the driver's seat, when I suddenly realised that in Great Britain the passenger always drives.

**5** I was burning my hands when I turned on the bathroom tap. Why do the British have one tap for hot water and one tap for cold?

**6** a) He drove his Ford at sixty mph when he had his fatal accident. b) She was driving her Ford at sixty kph when she had her fatal accident. *Who was the faster driver and who did the impossible?*

**7** I have been trying to brush up my phrasal verbs in England, when I came across a book called '1001 ways to avoid phrasal verbs'.

**8** I'd bought the best King Edwards potatoes, washed them, peeled them, boiled them for twenty minutes and mashed them when I found out she ate only rice.

**9** I had been expecting a call for ages. Leslie and Lesley had finally been ringing me at eight to invite me to their wedding. It was to be a traditional affair so I had to buy one of those large hats.

**10** I had waited until the weather man gave the temperature as 68 degrees Fahrenheit before I said that nobody except the British used Fahrenheit and 20 degrees C was the real temperature.

**11** a) I went to the bar and Andrew ordered a pint. b) I went to the bar and John had ordered a litre. *Who ordered first and who ordered more?*

**12** 'Morning, Sir Reginald. I'd seen you yesterday morning in your Rolls and you were driving on the wrong side of the road.' 'But my dear Luigi, in England the left is the right side of the road.'

**13** Waiter! You've brought me tea with a slice of lemon instead of milk. And what's that fly in my cup? It must be English – it had fallen in because it had a heart attack.

**14** The rest of Europe had a decimal system for centuries by the time the British changed from £.s.d. (pounds, shillings and pence).

**15** The last time I was in England I didn't try to balance peas on the back of my fork. I've tried it on a previous visit. I'm surprised the English don't starve to death.

# 2.19 – Story swop

## A  Girl had bullet in her scalp

For three months Sarah Hamilton had been walking around with a bullet in her head, thinking it was a sore.

Sarah, aged ten, of Ward End, Birmingham, was walking with a friend to a fish and chip shop in July when she felt a sharp pain on the crown of her head.

She thought she had been hit by a stone and, two days later, she saw a doctor who gave her ointment for the 'sore'.

But yesterday, as her brother, Paul, aged eighteen, washed her hair he saw a piece of metal sticking out of her head.

She was taken to a Birmingham hospital where doctors removed the bullet.

Police are trying to find who fired the .22 bullet.

After doctors had removed the missile, she said: 'Everyone has told me I've been very lucky.'

*The Times* (10.10.86)

© *The Times* 10.10.86

## B  Getting the wind up

Twenty-nine-year-old New Yorker Elvita Adams had been feeling extremely depressed for some time. She had decided to end it all and had taken the lift to the observation tower on the eighty-sixth floor of the Empire State Building. While she was standing looking out over the New York skyline, she suddenly flung herself from the tower with a piercing scream.

Seconds later, she was more or less back where she had started – a freak draught of air had plucked her from certain death. The thirty mile an hour gust had whipped her back up the face of the 1,472 foot high skyscraper and dropped her on the thirty inch wide concrete ledge on the eighty-fifth floor. Hearing her moans, security guard, Frank Clark opened the window and pulled her to safety inside.

Elvita who escaped with minor injuries and bruises said: 'I guess the good Lord didn't mean me to die just yet.'

*The Book of Narrow Escapes* (adapted)

## C  Head case

Mr Kenneth English, a salesman from Florida, USA, had been feeling depressed for some time. He had bought a gun and booked into a motel.

On his first evening in the motel, while he was sitting in his room, he made a sudden decision. He took out the gun he had purchased and shot himself in the head three times.

When he had woken up several hours later, he decided to go home. He explained away his bloodied head by telling his wife that he had been in a fight. Then he went off to bed.

The following morning, Mrs English drove her husband to hospital. There doctors discovered that all three bullets had passed clean through his head. They patched up the holes and sent him home with orders to rest.

Police later found all three bullets embedded in a wall in Mr English's motel room and charged him with criminal damage.

*The Book of Narrow Escapes* (adapted)

## D  The worst bank robbers

In August 1975, three men were entering a bank, when they got stuck in the revolving doors and had to be helped free by the staff.

They had been on their way to rob the Royal Bank of Scotland at Rothesay. They thanked everyone for their help and left.

A few minutes later they returned and announced their intention of robbing the bank but nobody believed them. First they demanded £5,000 but the head cashier only laughed at them, thinking it was a joke. The gang leader reduced his demand to £500, then to £50 and finally to 50 pence. Then one of the men jumped over the counter and hurt his ankle, while the other two got stuck in the doors again trying to make a getaway.

*The Book of Heroic Failures* (adapted)

# 3.1 – How simple is the future simple?

---

### Shall and will

*Will* is used with all persons but *shall* can be used as an alternative with *I* and *we* in pure future reference.

### Negative

*Will not* contracts to *'ll not* or *won't; shall not* contracts to *shan't.* . . .

In AmE *shan't* is rare and *shall* with a future reference is unusual.

*Longman English Grammar* L. G. Alexander

---

### *Will* against *shall* in future tenses

The question of which to use is not an important one. Apart from the fact that they are often contracted and therefore indistinguishable, it is seldom incorrect to use *will* with all persons (*I, we* as well as *she, you,* etc.).

*Grammar in Context* Hugh Gethin

---

I find myself following the traditional *shall/will* rules in writing and in formal speech; and not using the distinction in everyday conversation, where I don't think I ever use anything other than *will* or *'ll.*

David Crystal *English Today No. 5*

---

Negative statements and questions are also more common with *won't* than *shan't,* e.g. *We won't be able to come tomorrow* . . .

The 'classical' or 'simple' form of the future is usually given as;

| I<br>we | shall | you, he, she,<br>it, they | will |
|---|---|---|---|

The differences in meaning between *I/we shall* and *I/we will* are no longer clear, partly because we now use the short form -*'ll* for both, and partly because usage is different in different parts of the English speaking world (e.g. many Americans only use *will*).

*Cassell's Students' English Grammar*
Jake Allsop

---

1 There are two auxiliaries to form the future simple. **True/False?**
2 The auxiliaries contract in the same way in positive sentences. **True/False?**
3 There is only one contracted form of the future simple in the negative. **True/False?**
4 The British commonly use only one form of the future simple in negative contractions. **True/False?**
5 A distinction is always made between *I/we* and *you, he, she, it, they* with the future simple in spoken British English. **True/False?**
6 A distinction used to be made between *I, we* and *you, he, she, it, they* but it is disappearing, especially in English speaking countries outside England. **True/False?**
7 In British English there is still a tendency to use the old *I/we* and *you, he, she, it, they* rules in formal writing and speech. **True/False?**
8 Which popular newspaper has the 'correct' headline, *The Star* or *The Sun*?

# 3.2 – Funny future

## A Predictions

Write the verb form(s) used for the future in the box.

_____

**1**
A: What's the forecast?
B: The papers say it'll rain but the TV says it's going to be dry.
A: Hey! Forget the forecast, look at those clouds. Let's run for cover, it's going to rain.
B: Typical! In England it only rains between the showers.

**2**
A: Who do you think'll win the match?
B: Scandinavia.
A: What's your best subject– football or geography? You mean Sweden. I'm sorry but they're going to lose.
B: Look! There's no one defending the goal . . .! Sweden are going to win!
A: Don't be crazy! That's their own goal.

a) _will_ can be used for prediction **True/False?**
b) _going to_ can be used for prediction **True/False?**
c) _will_ can be used for something we can see now which is certain to happen **True/False?**
d) _going to_ can be used for something we can see now which is certain to happen **True/False?**

_will_ has many uses. In these examples is it used:

- to give an opinion? ☐
- to make a spontaneous decision? ☐
- to state a fact? ☐

## B Decisions

Write the verb form(s) used for the future in the box.

_____

**1**
A: I'm seeing the dentist later.
B: Really!
A: Yes, I'm having some wisdom teeth put in.
B: Is that your worst joke?

**2**
Any plans for tomorrow?
Yes, I'm going to explore the other side of the island.

**3**
WAITER: Can I take your order now?
CUSTOMER: Yes, I'm going to have ice cream. No, hang on a minute, I'll have apple pie without cream, please.
WAITER: Sorry, sir. We don't serve it with cream. We only serve it without.

Which of these decisions:
a) have already been made?
b) are being made now?

_will_ has many uses. In Example 3 is it used:

- to give an opinion? ☐
- to make a spontaneous decision? ☐
- to state a fact? ☐

## C Will

**1** This is the nine o'clock news. According to a White House spokesman, next week the superpowers will have more talks about future talks for a meeting to talk about discussing future talks.

*will* has many uses. In these examples, is it used:

- to give an opinion? ☐
- to make a spontaneous decision? ☐
- to state a fact? ☐

**2** 'He'll be a year old at Easter.'

## D Look it up

**1**

**THE BOER WAR**

In 1999 South Africa celebrates the centenary of The Boer War.

**2**

# RAMADAN

This year Ramadan, the holy month of the Muslim calendar, starts in July. As they have a lunar calendar, the months are at different times each year.

**3**

# Kenya/ Tanzania Safari

### DAY 2
### AMBOSELI

Our Safari begins by driving south to Amboseli National Park. This park at the foot of Mount Kilimanjaro is home to Wildebeast, Zebra and Antelope with their attendant predators. Lunch is followed by a game drive. Dinner and overnight at Amboseli Lodge.

**4**

# Lake Lucerne

**Days 3 to 6 At leisure in Lützelau with included excursions**. There are plenty of excursions planned for your enjoyment. There's an included excursion to Interlaken through the towering mountains of the Bernese Oberland by glittering lakes to the Brünig Pass – it was near here at Reichenbach Falls that Dr. Moriarty flung Sherlock Holmes to his presumed death! You return by Brienz, home of Swiss woodcarving. You will also have a full day in Lucerne. Optional excursions include a cable car ride to 10,000 ft. up Mt. Titlis, a trip to Lake Lugano, a mountain excursion to three dramatic passes and a Swiss folklore evening.

**5**

## NEW LONDON
Drury Lane, WC2B 5PW
Map reference B3
**Box Office** (CC) 405 0072/404 4079
**Groups** 930 6123/405 1567

The ANDREW LLOYD WEBBER
T.S. ELIOT
International Award Winning Musical      MUSICAL

## Cats

Booking to September. Some seats available
for eve perfs and Tues mats from June
Singles available from May
Mon-Sat at 7.45, Mats Tues and Sat at 3.00
Prices: £7.00-£25.00
Eve perf ends approx at 10.30

When does this evening's performance start?

**6**

Our hovercraft gets in at 17.45 this evening

| Departure Days | | Flight No. | SNCF Train No. | Dep. Paris Nord | Dep. Amiens | Arr. Boulogne Hov'port | Dep. Boulogne Hov'port | Arr. Dover Hov'port | Dep. Dover | Arr. London Victoria | |
|---|---|---|---|---|---|---|---|---|---|---|---|
| 01/05/90 to | Daily | 824 | 2009 | 0854 | 1000 | 1112 | 1205 | 1145 | 1240 | 1406 | All times are local. The time in France is one hour ahead of that in the UK except between 30 Sept and 27 Oct when times are the same. |
| 29/09/90 | Daily | 835 | 2017 | 1121 | 1233 | 1340 | 1405 | 1345 | 1455* | 1624* | |
| | Daily | 846 | 2023 | 1312 | 1422 | 1530 | 1605 | 1545 | 1655* | 1824* | **Bank Holidays in England/Wales** |
| | Daily | 861 | 2029 | 1620 | 1730 | 1845 | 1905 | 1845 | 1940* | 2106* | 7, 28 May; 27 August. |
| 30/09/90 to | Daily | 824 | 2009 | 0854 | 1000 | 1112 | 1205 | 1245 | 1340 | 1506 | **Bank Holidays in France** |
| 27/10/90 | Daily | 835 | 2017 | 1121 | 1233 | 1340 | 1405 | 1445 | 1555 | 1724 | 1, 8, 24 May; 4 June; |
| | Daily | 851 | 2025 | 1417 | 1524 | 1640 | 1705 | 1745 | 1840 | 2006 | 14 July; 15 August. |

**7**

## ROYAL ENGAGEMENTS

**The Queen**, accompanied by **The Duke of Edinburgh**, attends the Maundy Service in Birmingham Cathedral, and distributes the Royal Maundy during the service; lunches with the Lord Mayor of Birmingham at the Council House; and, later, opens the New Halls development of the National Exhibition Centre, Birmingham.
'The Independent'

Sort these texts into three categories:

| X | Y | Z |
|---|---|---|
| | | |
| | | |

Can you work out what X, Y and Z stand for?

# Summary tables

| decisions already made | future as fact | prediction: certain to happen |

| prediction | spontaneous decisions |

## Table 1

| Example sentence | Verb form | Use |
|---|---|---|
| 1 The paper says it'll rain. | | |
| 2 The TV says it's going to rain. | | |
| 3 There's no one defending the goal. Sweden is going to win. | | |
| 4 I'm seeing the dentist later. | | |
| 5 I'm going to explore the other side of the island. | | |
| 6 No, hang on a minute, I'll have apple pie. | | |
| 7 The superpowers will have more talks about future talks... | | |
| 8 This year Ramadan starts in July. | | |

## Table 2

| Verb form | Uses |
|---|---|
| 1 *will* | |
| 2 *going to* | |
| 3 present continuous | |
| 4 present simple | |

a)  There is only one verb form used to talk about the future    **True/False?**

b)  The verb form you choose depends on how you want to see the future.    **True/False?**

# 3.3 – Journalist of the future

**Uses** | future as fact    decision already made    spontaneous decision    prediction |

**Verb forms** | going to    present simple    future simple    present continuous |

| LE MONDE | PRAVDA |
|---|---|
| **CHUNNEL NEXT STEP** | **SOVIET-AMERICAN TALKS** |
| Use<br>Verb form | Use<br>Verb Form |
|  |  |

| FOLHA DE SÃO PAULO | THE INDIAN TIMES |
|---|---|
| **PRESIDENT'S TERM IS UP** | **FILMSTAR'S FUTURE** |
| Use<br>Verb form | Use<br>Verb form |
|  | 'I ...................................................................<br><br>...................................................................,'<br><br>said Soria, India's top actress. |

| AL AHRAM | THE TIMES |
|---|---|
| **BEIRUT AIRPORT TO REOPEN** | **TODAY'S WEATHER** |
| Use<br>Verb form | Use<br>Verb form |
|  |  |

# 3.4 – Double date

| **Bill** | **Henrietta** |
|---|---|
| *Wednesday* | *Wednesday* |
| 12<br>6<br>7<br>8<br>11 | 12<br>3<br>6<br>7<br>9<br>10 |

| **Tom** | **Edward** |
|---|---|
| *Wednesday* | *Wednesday* |
| 12 Lunch – Edward (unconfirmed)<br>5 squash (to be arranged)<br>6 Mary + Henrietta at cinema<br>7 ring Bill<br>8 jogging cancelled<br>10 overseas call from USA expected | 12<br>3<br>6<br>8<br>10 |

| **Bill** | **Henrietta** |
|---|---|
| *Wednesday* | *Wednesday* |
| 12<br>6<br>7<br>8<br>11 | 12 business lunch<br>3 call Tom<br>6 Bill at restaurant<br>7 dinner with Mum and dad<br>9 hairdressers - dye hair<br>10 walk dog |

| **Tom** | **Edward** |
|---|---|
| *Wednesday* | *Wednesday* |
| 12<br>5<br>6<br>7<br>8<br>10 | 12<br>3<br>6<br>8<br>10 |

# Double date 2

**Bill**

*Wednesday*

12
6
7
8
11

**Henrietta**

*Wednesday*

12
3
6
7
9
10

**Tom**

*Wednesday*

12
5
6
7
8
10

**Edward**

*Wednesday*

12 lunch - Tom (to be confirmed)
3 pick up car (first check with garage)
6 dinner at "Luigi's"
8 Henrietta after cinema
10 Heathrow airport - stepmother
Terminal 1

**Bill**

*Wednesday*

12 lunch - no plans
6 coffee with Henrietta
7 pick up plants from nursery
8 Supper Jean + Arthur
11 documentary on TV

**Henrietta**

*Wednesday*

12
3
6
7
9
10

**Tom**

*Wednesday*

12
5
6
7
8
10

**Edward**

*Wednesday*

12
3
6
8
10

# 3.5 – Anyone for cricket?

CURIOUS
VISITOR: (1) How do you play cricket?

CRICKET
FAN: (2) I'll try to explain it to you:
You have two sides, one out in the field and one in. Each man that's in the side that's in goes out and when he's out he comes in and the next man goes in until he's out. When they're all out, the side that's out comes in and the side that's been in goes out and tries to get those coming in out. Sometimes you get players still in and not out. When both sides have been in and out including the not outs, that's the end of the game.

VISITOR: (3) Listen, let's go and see a match. Then I understand it better.

## At the match

FAN: (4) First you should know that there are two teams, each with eleven players.

VISITOR: (5) Hey, the man with the stick isn't playing very well, is he?

FAN: (6) You mean the batsman – and it's a bat, not a stick. But you're right, I think he's making a mistake in a minute, the ball is hitting his wicket and then he'll be out.

VISITOR: (7) What are the wickets?

FAN: (8) The three pieces of wood the batsman must defend. Hey, you're not bored, are you?

VISITOR: (9) Well, a little bit. It's confusing with bats and wickets and bowling. Why do they bowl the ball? Throwing it would be easier.

FAN: (10) Don't worry, we're leaving at six.

VISITOR: (11) At six! How long does a cricket match last?

FAN: (12) Up to five days.

VISITOR: (13) You mean the match'll continue for another four days?!

FAN: (14) Yes, if the weather stays fine.

VISITOR: (15) What's the forecast?

FAN: (16) It rains tomorrow.

VISITOR: (17) I think you'll have to explain a lot more before I understand anything about cricket.

FAN: (18) Don't worry, I explain it to you when they have afternoon tea.

VISITOR: (19) Are they going to have afternoon tea! Oh, how English! Hey, the bowler has hit the wicket.

FAN: (20) That's the whole idea. He probably does it again soon. But as it's now teatime, I'll tell you what happens from the beginning.

VISITOR: (21) You mean you are explaining the game to me again?! Well, firstly, I'll tell you what'll happen in a minute. See those dark clouds – it's raining very soon. When's the next match?

FAN: (22) It starts in two weeks. There are five altogether.

VISITOR: (23) It sounds like a war rather than a sport.

# 3.6 – Who will be dancing in the streets?

**1** People will be wearing tropical costumes and strange masks and men will be dressing up as women.

**2** Do you know will the police be dancing in the streets when they are on duty over the last weekend of August?

**3** Won't they be dancing to reggae music as well?

**4** Once again they will be celebrate this annual event in the streets.

**5** The poor will imitating the rich and the royals.

**6** The police will be being searched by the public for drugs and weapons.

**7** Will not the steelbands be playing their famous pan music?

**Steelband instruments**
There are four main types of pan instruments:

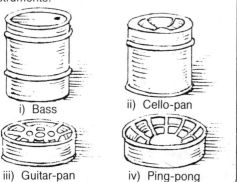

i) Bass    ii) Cello-pan

iii) Guitar-pan    iv) Ping-pong

**8** Nobody will be working until Tuesday, isn't it?

**9** Will be coming one million people to see it, like last year?

**10** As usual it'll be dramatising social and political events.

**11** We shan't be going to bed for forty-eight hours.

## Substitution table

| | Europe's biggest street festival |
|---|---|
| | Next weekend in Notting Hill (just north of Hyde Park) about one million people, many of them from London's Caribbean community, |
| **Positive** | \_\_\_\_\_ \_\_\_\_\_ ce\_\_\_\_\_ Carnival, or Mas as it's called in Trinidad, the |
| **Positive contraction** | They \_\_\_\_\_ \_\_\_\_\_ country of its origin. |
| **Negative** | The police \_\_\_\_\_ \_\_\_\_\_ \_\_\_\_\_ ta\_\_\_\_\_ their duties seriously unless of course |
| **Negative contraction** | \_\_\_\_\_ \_\_\_\_\_ ta\_\_\_\_\_ crimes are committed. |
| **Positive question** | \_\_\_\_\_ they \_\_\_\_\_ da\_\_\_\_\_ in the streets with the public? |
| **Negative question** | \_\_\_\_\_ they \_\_\_\_\_ da\_\_\_\_\_ |

# 3.7 – Gilbert

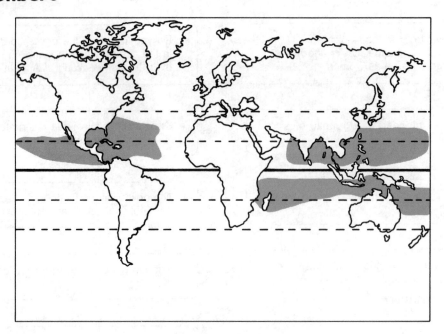

KINGSTON, JAMAICA

NEWSFLASH
The Office of Disaster Preparedness has just issued
the following warning: Hurricane Gilbert is
approaching Jamaica and is reported to be one of
the worst hurricanes this century. Everybody is
advised not to leave their homes and to board up
all windows. We'll be reporting on Gilbert's
progress in a special programme between 10.00 and
10.30 later tonight.

NEWSFLASH
The latest forecast says Gilbert will be reaching
the Jamaican coast at 3 am. As most people will be
sleeping when it hits the island, they are advised
to cover all windows, to secure any possessions
outdoors before going to bed, and not to go outside
at any time during the storm.

We now go over to the Met Office for the background
story on Gilbert. Well, as the hurricane passes
over, winds will gust up to an incredible 266kph.
However, as the eye of the storm approaches, the
sky will brighten and the wind will drop for an
hour before the other half of the storm hits land.

Why is it that Jamaica and the Caribbean region
are the victims of hurricanes whereas many other
parts of the world escape such disasters? Well,
there are six regions in the world where hurricanes
develop and these are restricted to tropical ocean
areas. So it seems Jamaica will always be having
cyclones and hurricanes.

1 Is the report regarded as a *period* or *point of time*?

2 Is the arrival of the hurricane seen as an *action in progress in the future*?

3 Are most people expected to go to sleep before or after Gilbert arrives?

4 Is the future incidence of hurricanes seen as likely to be frequent or extremely frequent?

# 3.8 – Caribbean future

| interrupted action | | emphasising very frequent action |
|---|---|---|

| action at/around a point of time | | action through a period |
|---|---|---|

| Example sentence | Use | Timeline |
|---|---|---|
| 1 We'll be reporting on Gilbert's progress in a special programme between ten and ten thirty later tonight. | | |
| 2 Gilbert will be reaching the Jamaican coast at three a.m. | | |
| 3 Most people will be sleeping when it hits the island. | | |
| 4 Jamaica will always be having cyclones and hurricanes. | | |

When a speaker chooses the future continuous to describe an action, it is because they see it in progress. **True/False?**

## Contrasting future simple and future continuous

1 a) We'll be reporting on Gilbert's progress from ten to ten thirty.
  b) We'll report on Gilbert's progress from ten to ten thirty.

  i) a) and b) have the same meaning objectively. **True/False?**
  ii) In which sentence does the announcer see the programme extended in time?

2 a) Gilbert will be reaching the Jamaican coast at three a.m.
  b) Gilbert will reach the Jamaican coast at three a.m.

Does the speaker see a) or b) as an action in progress?

3 a) Most people will be sleeping when it hits the island.
  b) Most people will sleep when it hits the island.

Which situation is extremely unlikely?

4 a) Jamaica will always be having cyclones and hurricanes.
  b) Jamaica will always have cyclones and hurricanes.

Which report emphasises the high incidence of cyclones and hurricanes?

# 3.9 – Siesta

siesta

underground
shelter

a carnation
in my jacket

transcendental
meditation

15,000 metres

**I** How will I recognise you at
the station?

**2** Whatever you do, don't
come at six this evening!

**3** What about the altitude
during the flight?

**4** I've won £1,000,000!

**5** The number one tennis seed
has withdrawn from the
tournament.

**6** Could you drop in a little
later than eleven a.m.?

**7** I wouldn't ring our Spanish
branch immediately after
lunch!

**8** And now we go over to our
correspondent in America
for a live broadcast.

**9** My neighbour has hit another
lamp post!

**10** What if they drop a nuclear
bomb?

one million
spectators/when
shuttle launch

Wimbledon

brunch

accidents

money problems

# 3.10 – The perfect future for the kangaroo?

## The shooting continues

**1770:**  'What is it?' said one of the first
English visitors to an Australian
Aborigine (who had never heard
English spoken before), when he saw
5  a strange animal. 'Kangaroo?' was the
answer, which of course means,
'What did you say?' in the native
language. The Englishman thought it
was the name of the animal. The
10  mistake has never been corrected,
but things have changed a lot since
that day.

**1997:**  By the end of this year the 3,100 professional kangaroo shooters in
Australia will have shoot dead another three million kangaroos. In recent
15  years population estimates have varied from twenty to sixty million animals,
which means there are, at the moment, more kangaroos than people – the
population of Australia is fifteen million. But how long will this last?

Many non-professionals will also have be shooting kangaroos illegally.
So the unofficial number that will has be shot will be much higher
20  than the annual figure of three million.

Australia has forty-seven species of kangaroo, but many fear that in a short
time, three of them, the Big Red, the Eastern Grey, and the Western
Grey will died out. Of the millions shot, how many 'll 've been hit but
not killed? The cruelty and suffering is on a terrible scale.

25  By 1997 the Europeans will have only lived in Australia for just over
two hundred years – the first settlement was in 1788. How many
thousands of years will have been living there the kangaroo?

Why so many people will once again have been ignore this annual
massacre for the whole year is difficult to understand. Many dogs
30  will probably have eaten kilos of kangaroo meat by the end of this
year, hasn't it? Don't people know that most countries buy kangaroo
meat for pet food?

By the end of the year many joeys (baby kangaroos) won't have found
their parents because they will have disappeared and their skin will
35  have been made into purses, rugs, toys, coats, and endless souvenirs.
How many more kangaroos must die before the shooting stops?

# Substitution table

## Future perfect simple

| | |
|---|---|
| Positive<br>Positive contraction<br><br>Negative<br>Negative contraction | By the end of the year { they _____ _____ s_____ another three million kangaroos.<br><br>the shooting _____ _____ _____  st _____<br>_____ _____ |
| Positive question<br>Negative question | _____ _____ the kangaroo _____ b_____ extinct by 2000?<br>_____ |
| Passive<br>Passive question | By the end of the year three million _____ _____ _____ s_____ .<br>_____ all the kangaroos _____ _____ s_____ by 2000? |

## Future perfect continuous

| | |
|---|---|
| Positive<br>Positive contraction | By the end of the night they _____ _____ _____ hun_____ for eight hours<br>_____ continuously. |
| Negative<br>Negative contraction | It is still dusk so they _____ _____ _____ _____ sh_____ for very long.<br>_____ |
| Positive question<br>Negative question<br>Negative contraction | By the end of the season { how many kangaroos _____ _____ _____ ly_____ wounded before they die.<br>why _____ the public _____ _____ _____ tr_____ to stop the massacre?<br>why _____ the public _____ _____ tr_____ to stop the massacre? |

# 3.11 – 2001 and the ozone story

## Mini-texts

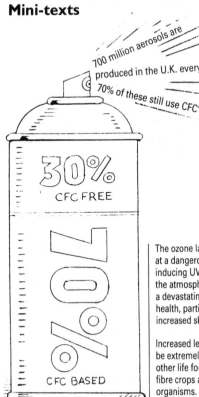

700 million aerosols are produced in the U.K. every year

70% of these still use CFC'S.

**30% CFC FREE**

**70% CFC BASED**

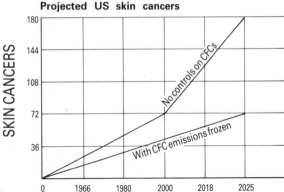

### Projected US skin cancers

No controls on CFCs

With CFC emissions frozen

SKIN CANCERS

180
144
108
72
36

0    1966    1980    2000    2018    2025

YEARS

The ozone layer in the atmosphere allows life on Earth to flourish. It absorbs damaging ultraviolet radiation (UV-B) from the sun.

The ozone layer is now thinning out at a dangerous rate. More cancer-inducing UV-B is getting through the atmosphere, and this will have a devastating impact on human health, particularly in terms of increased skin cancers.

Increased levels of UV-B will also be extremely damaging to many other life forms, including cereals, fibre crops and sensitive marine organisms.

The damage to the ozone layer is being done by chemicals called chlorofluorocarbons (CFCs) which are used in a wide range of industrial processes.

What's more, CFCs will accelerate the process of 'global warming', which will in turn have a profoundly disturbing impact on climate patterns and terrestrial eco-systems.

The biggest single use of CFCs is as propellants in aerosol sprays. In the US, they were banned for this purpose back in 1978. Other major uses are in foam packaging, (in hamburger cartons, for instance), air conditioning units and refrigerants.

The amount of CFCs currently released into the atmosphere is currently six times greater than can actually be absorbed.

Because it takes so long to remove CFCs from the atmosphere, an 85% reduction is needed just to stabilise the ozone layer at current levels.

There are substitutes and alternatives available for almost all uses of the most dangerous kinds of CFC.

Once up in the atmosphere (where they can last for up to 100 years) CFCs release chlorine. A single molecule of chlorine can destroy 100,000 molecules of ozone.

1  In 1987 an international agreement to limit CFC production was signed. In September 1999 this agreement will have been in force for twelve years. With measures such as these industrialists expect that by the year 2000 we will have just avoided a global catastrophe.

2  Scientific discoveries are often made suddenly and contrary to expectations. Manufacturers are already building plants at a cost of millions of pounds to produce a harmless substitute for CFCs. By the end of the century we will have found a simple and dramatic solution to the problem of the ozone layer.

3  A hole has appeared in the ozone layer over the Antarctic. It has been gradually growing and now covers an area the size of the USA. Environmentalists fear that more and more such holes will have appeared by the year 2000 and that the ozone layer will no longer protect the planet.

1  a)  The start of the agreement is in the *past/present/future*?
   b)  Will the agreement still be in force in 1999?
   c)  Is the catastrophe expected to be avoided *a short time before the end of the century,
       at the turn of the century*, or *after the turn of the century*?

2  When exactly between now and the end of the century is the solution expected to be found?

3  In this example the future perfect simple is used to talk about *a single action/several actions*?

# 3.12 – Ozone – a thing of the past or the future?

A  Write the following uses of the future perfect simple in the table.  B  Complete timelines for them

| action repeated at indefinite times in a future period |
| action completed shortly before a future point |

| situation extending over a future period |
| action completed at an indefinite time in a future period |

| Example sentence | Use | Timeline |
|---|---|---|
| 1 In September 1999 the agreement will have been in force for twelve years. | | |
| 2 By the year 2000 we will have just avoided a catastrophe. | | |
| 3 By the end of the century we will have found a simple solution to the problem of the ozone layer. | | |
| 4 Environmentalists fear that more and more holes will have appeared by the year 2000. | | |

## C  Contrasting future perfect simple and future simple

1  a) In September 1999 the agreement will have been in force for twelve years.
   b) From September 1999 the agreement will be in force for twelve years.

What is the difference?

2  a) By the year 2000 we will have just avoided a catastrophe.
   b) In the year 2000 we will just avoid a catastrophe.

What is the difference?

3  a) By the end of the century we will have found a solution.
   b) By the end of the century we will find a solution.

Which sentence emphasises the completion of the action?

4  a) People fear that more holes will have appeared by 2000.
   b) People fear that more holes will appear in 2000.

Which holes will appear first, those in a) or b)?

# 3.13 – By the time you're 100 ...

Assuming you're an average English person, then by the time you're 100 ...

**1 Potatoes**

93 kilos
930 kilos
9,300 kilos
93,000 kilos

**2 Sleep**

1 year
5 years
17 years
29 years
42 years

**3 Tea Tea Tea Tea Tea**

37,111 cups of tea
62,004 cups of tea
99,700 cups of tea
169,725 cups of tea
450,000 cups of tea

**4 TV addicts**

56,568 hours
112,270 hours
207,911 hours
502,644 hours

**5 Read, read, read**

*newspapers*

The Sun
The Guardian          982
The Star             4770
The Observer        31,025
The Daily Telegraph 52,118
The Times
The Independent

**6 Days of rain**

1,111 days
2,222 days
3,333 days
4,444 days

**7 Use the word *get***

7,081
70,810
708,100
7,081,000  ...  times!!

*get up get in get on get over get out get down get, get, get, get, get, get,*

**8 Cat or dog food**

£5,000
£12,000
£33,000
£40,000

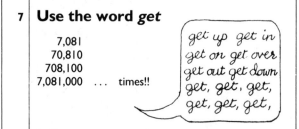

**9 Distance**

by car on the
*left*-hand side
of the road

150,000 miles
264,000,000 yards
9,504,000,000 inches

# 3.14 – Problems, problems, problems!

**1**  A:  I can't open the door!
   B:  It'll be alright – just hang on a few more minutes.
   A:  But we can't wait, we'll drown!
   B:  No, it'll be OK. When it's full up with water, we'll be able to open the door.

> seeping  by  enough  The  in  for  have
> water  long  will  been  then.

a)  Is the water seeping in at the time of the conversation?
b)  Did the water start seeping in before the conversation began?
c)  Will it continue to seep in?
d)  *by then* means . . .?

**2**  A:  (on the phone) What shall I do?
   B:  You'll have to break the door.
     Don't try to push anything into his mouth; just try and keep him still.

> you  When  in  get,  probably  he  his
> been  just  swallowing  have  tongue.  will

a)  *B will enter the room./The man will swallow his tongue.*
    Which will happen first?
b)  How much time will there be between the two actions?
c)  Which word tells us that?

**3**  A:  When is it?
   B:  Next Thursday – three o'clock.
   A:  And how many's that?
   B:  Twelve! One every six months!
   A:  Be careful with the three-point turn this time!
   B:  Just think.

> I'll  tests  six  next  for  by  have  taking
> been  years  Thursday!

a)  When did he start having tests?
b)  Will he have any more?
c)  Is he talking about a single action or several repeated actions?
d)  Is he thinking about a point of time or a period of time?

# 3.15 – Perfection at last

| action completed shortly before a future point | actions repeated in a period before a future point |
|---|---|

| action continuing up to a future point |
|---|

| Example sentence | Use | Timeline |
|---|---|---|
| **1** Wait a few more minutes. The water will have been seeping in for long enough by then. | | |
| **2** When you get in, he will have just been swallowing his tongue. | | |
| **3** I'll have been taking tests for six years by next Thursday. | | |

When a speaker chooses the future perfect continuous, he or she sees a situation which is in progress extending up to a point in the future.     **True/False?**

## Contrasting future perfect simple and future perfect continuous

1 a) The water will have been seeping in for five minutes by then.
   b) The water will have seeped in for five minutes by then.

   c) When you get in, he will have just been swallowing his tongue.
   d) When you get in, he will have just swallowed his tongue.

   e) I'll have been taking tests for six years by next Thursday.
   f) I'll have taken tests for six years by next Thursday.

i) The above pairs of sentences have the same meaning objectively.     **True/False?**
ii) In which sentences are the situations seen as extended actions?

# 3.16 – What future?

At the present rate of destruction the Amazon forests will be gone within 30 years. **Norman Myers** on the coming of catastrophe

ACCORDING to Nasa scientists, the last three months (July–September) have seen even more burning of tropical forest in eastern and southern parts of Brazilian Amazonia than in 1987, when a whopping 32,000 square miles went up in smoke. And this is in just certain sectors of the region.

When we add in other parts of Brazilian Amazonia, plus those parts of Amazonia in Colombia, Peru and Ecuador, the total could well be more than 50,000 square miles, or 3.6 per cent of the region. If deforestation continues at this rate, and even without any speeding up of the process, all Amazonia's forests would disappear within a few years.

1 Be quick or else when you go to visit the Amazon, the forests will already go.

2 It has been recently predicted that the Amazon forests will disappear within the next thirty years.

3 They will cut down and burn all the trees by the time you come.

4 The inhabitants of the Amazon region will be living in a desert before they finally realise what has happened.

5 Many people will expect the disaster when it comes.

6 They will destroy thousands of unique plants, insects and animals by the year 2000.

7 By 2000 the amount of carbon dioxide in the atmosphere will have been increasing dramatically since twenty years.

8 It is our problem because when they'll have finished burning the forest, you and I won't have sufficient oxygen to breathe.

9 We can't ignore the problem because in ten years time the greenhouse effect will have become a global phenomenon.

10 You can have this article in a few minutes because I will have been reading it by then.

# 3.17 – Futuristic city?: Text A

Some say that it now stands at sixteen million, others say that nineteen million is nearer the true figure. It is difficult to be precise but the frightening fact is that in the year 2000 the population of Mexico City will be reaching thirty million.

And that is not the only problem. City planners know that major changes must be made – and made quickly – to provide more water. Otherwise it is conceivable that the water supply in the city will have run out by 1995.

And there is worse. By the year 2000 the city will have been slowly sinking for twenty years. Originally the whole city area was a lake and the earth which was used to fill it cannot support the weight of large buildings. In spite of this and even though the whole area suffers from earthquakes, building continues.

However, the greatest tragedy of all is that at the turn of the century many people will already be dying from pollution-related diseases. Currently there are 12,000 tons of gaseous waste poisoning the air each day.

Mexico City is a modern city but it is a city almost out of control. It must be taken as a warning by the rest of the world as to what can and will happen when city planning cannot keep up with population growth.

---

1 In the year 2000 the population will be:

a) almost 30 million ☐

b) 30 million ☐

2 It is possible that there will be no water in the city:

a) in 1994 ☐

b) sometime in 1995 ☐

3 The sinking of the city will start:

a) in the year 2000 ☐

b) in 1980 ☐

c) before 2000 but we don't know ☐
exactly when

4 The sinking of the city by another 30 cm will happen:

a) before the year 2000 ☐

b) in the year 2000 ☐

c) no information ☐

5 The amount of gaseous waste is:

a) 12,000 tons each day ☐

b) will soon be 12,000 tons each day ☐

6 Deaths caused by pollution will happen:

a) only at the turn of the century ☐

b) before the turn of the century ☐

# Futuristic city?: Text B

Some commentators say that its population now numbers sixteen million, others believe that nineteen million is a truer estimate. However, the disturbing fact is that by the year 2000 the number of people living in Mexico City will have reached thirty million.

Water shortage is another problem facing the city. City planners are aware that measures must be taken quickly, otherwise it is possible that the city's water supply will run out in 1995.

And there is a further problem. By the year 2000 the city will have sunk another thirty cm or more. The whole area used to be a lake filled in with earth which today cannot support the weight of modern buildings. Yet, building still continues, and this is in spite of the fact that the area is prone to earthquakes.

More tragic still is the fact that at the turn of the century many people will start dying from pollution-related diseases. 12,000 tons of gaseous waste poison the atmosphere each day.

Mexico City is a modern city almost out of control. As such it must stand as a warning to the city planners and developers in the rest of the world as to what may and will happen when a city cannot keep pace with its own population growth.

1 In the year 2000 the population will be:

a) almost 30 million ☐

b) 30 million ☐

2 It is possible that there will be no water in the city:

a) in 1994 ☐

b) sometime in 1995 ☐

3 The sinking of the city will start:

a) in the year 2000 ☐

b) in 1980 ☐

c) before 2000 but we don't know exactly when ☐

4 The sinking of the city by another 30 cm will happen:

a) before the year 2000 ☐

b) in the year 2000 ☐

c) no information ☐

5 The amount of gaseous waste is:

a) 12,000 tons each day ☐

b) will soon be 12,000 tons each day ☐

6 Deaths caused by pollution will happen:

a) only at the turn of the century ☐

b) before the turn of the century ☐